A Student Workbook for
COUNSELING ACROSS CULTURES

A Student Workbook for COUNSELING ACROSS CULTURES

Paul B. Pedersen
and
Daniel Hernández

UNIVERSITY OF HAWAII PRESS
HONOLULU

© 1993 University of Hawaii Press
All rights reserved

ISBN 0-8248-1524-6

Printed in the United States of America

98 97 96 95 94 93   5 4 3 2 1

```
616.8914 P371s

Pedersen, Paul, 1936-

A student workbook for
  Counseling across cultures
```

University of Hawaii books are printed on acid-free paper and meet the guidelines for
permanence and durability of the Council on Library Resources

CONTENTS

Introduction ... vii

1. Dilemmas and Choices in Cross-Cultural Counseling: The Universal versus the Culturally Distinctive ... 1

2. Client, Counselor, and Contextual Variables in Multicultural Counseling ... 7

3. Racism in Counseling as an Adversive Behavioral Process ... 13

4. Cross-Cultural Psychotherapy ... 19

5. Ethics in Multicultural Counseling ... 24

6. A Model for Counseling Asian Americans ... 30

7. Counseling the Hispanic Client: A Theoretical and Applied Perspective ... 34

8. Providing Counseling Services for Native American Indians: Client, Counselor, and Community Characteristics ... 39

9. Counseling Foreign Students ... 44

10. Counseling Refugees: The North American Experience ... 52

11. Behavioral Approaches to Counseling across Cultures ... 57

12. Assessment in Cross-Cultural Counseling ... 63

13. Research and Research Hypotheses about Effectiveness in Intercultural Counseling ... 73

Answer Key to Multiple Choice Questions ... 82

INTRODUCTION

The number of courses in multicultural counseling is increasing rapidly around the country. Many instructors are learning to teach about multicultural counseling from the great variety of textbooks and teaching materials now available. This workbook and student guide is an attempt to help students who are using *Counseling across Cultures,* Third Edition, by Paul B. Pedersen, Juris G. Draguns, Walter J. Lonner, and Joseph E. Trimble (Honolulu: University of Hawaii Press, 1989).

Each chapter of this workbook and student guide corresponds with a chapter in *Counseling across Cultures,* Third Edition. The authors of each chapter were consulted regarding each of the teaching aids provided in this book. Each chapter of this book is presented in a four-part format, consisting of discussion questions, multiple choice questions, case studies, and classroom activities.

Discussion Questions

Ten general discussion questions are provided for each chapter. These discussion questions have been selected to highlight some of the basic underlying themes or controversies in the chapter. The questions might be useful to promote class discussion, to set up a classroom debate, or to help the student identify issues in the chapter.

We have found the questions especially useful in a "take-home" format so that students can be looking for the answers to the essay questions while they are reading the chapter. In this way the student becomes more of a participant in a "discussion" with the chapter authors while reading the chapter. The discussion questions then become both a guide to the student's reading as well as test questions to measure the student's understanding of the chapter.

The discussion questions can be used to promote classroom discussion in small groups or in one large group. A debate might be organized on two sides of a particular issue among students in the classroom using one or more of the questions. Debates have been used in other multicultural counseling classes with considerable success.

Multiple Choice Questions

Ten multiple choice questions are provided for each chapter. These questions were designed to help the student test specific knowledge derived from the chapter.

Case Studies

Short critical incidents are provided that illustrate basic concepts within each chapter. These brief case examples are provided so that students can see the practical application of those concepts. The key ideas are not always immediately apparent in the case study, so the student's task is to "spot the concept" within the case study or critical incident.

The case studies may also be a springboard for class discussion about a particular case in small or large groups. It may even be possible to role-play the case in the group, with students taking on the roles in a psychodrama format.

The critical incidents may be followed by alternative choices, each one being acceptable but one being better than the others for a particular reason. Being able to pick the best choice will test the student's ability to understand the dynamics underlying each incident with regard to the chapter topic.

Students can use the critical incidents as models for other incidents in the real world outside the classroom. Students may collect their own examples of critical incidents from what they read or observe in daily life and bring these incidents to class for discussion.

Classroom Activities

A variety of classroom activities is provided that will suggest things students can do to experience some of the dynamics discussed in each chapter. These activities have been useful in teaching multicultural counseling. Instructors and students should feel free to modify any of the activities to fit their own unique needs and priorities. The activities can be useful for more than one chapter by modifying them to use with a different problem, issue, or target audience.

Students may wish to develop their own activities modeled on those presented here. The design of classroom activities is itself an appropriate and exciting activity. Using these examples may encourage students to demonstrate their own creativity.

The activities can be modified for collecting data that can be discussed in class and analyzed. The data might result in a classroom project or even publication. The activity may be carried out in class or with a population outside the classroom.

The objective of this workbook and student guide is to stimulate thinking about counseling across cultures in practical ways. The questions and activities are designed to enhance learning in the classroom and to help students realize the exciting opportunities that arise when the functions of counseling in multicultural settings are examined.

The following activities were included from *A Manual of Structured Experiences for Cross-Cultural Learning*, by W. Weeks, P. Pedersen, and R. Brislin (Yarmouth, Maine: Intercultural Press, 1977), by permission.

    The Multicultural Person
    Stereotypes (p. 26)
    The Hidden Agenda
    Role-Playing a Problem in a Group
    World Picture Test
    No Questions Asked
    Role-Playing a Newspaper Incident
    A Free Drawing Test
    Cross-Cultural Training Exercise for Interpreting Policy
    Cultural Value Systems with Conflicting Points of View
    Orientation for a Cross-Cultural Experience
    Dialogue within Ourselves
    Projecting into a Group
    Cross-Cultural Trade-Off
    Lump Sum

A Student Workbook for
COUNSELING ACROSS CULTURES

CHAPTER 1

DILEMMAS AND CHOICES IN CROSS-CULTURAL COUNSELING: THE UNIVERSAL VERSUS THE CULTURALLY DISTINCTIVE

The first chapter, by Juris G. Draguns, introduces the basic themes that cut across the theories and methods of cross-cultural counseling. This chapter provides a framework to organize the unique aspects of cross-cultural counseling and fit those aspects to the generic perspectives of counseling.

Discussion Questions

1. Describe three contrasting definitions of culture, pointing out the strengths and weaknesses of each one.

2. In what ways is the concept of counseling a product of a particular cultural perspective?

3. Discuss Patterson's contention that rejects "cross-culturalism" in favor of a universalistic perspective.

4. Discuss the two main approaches to cross-cultural research and the strengths or weaknesses of each.

5. Under what conditions would it be appropriate to change the environment rather than the person?

6. Discuss the relative importance of "relationship" and "technique" in cross-cultural counseling.

7. Define and discuss the terms "emic" and "etic."

8. Define and discuss the terms "alloplastic" and "autoplastic."

9. What are the social forces that have made counseling more responsive to cultural differences in society?

10. What research resources are available to the cross-cultural counselor?

Multiple Choice Questions

1. Families seeking temporary employment who experience stress due to readaptation in host countries are called:
   a) minority groups
   b) economically disadvantaged
   c) sojourners
   d) opportunist

2. Groups in the United States who are not considered "people of color" but whose language, customs, and identities are linked with their ancestral cultures in Europe and elsewhere are referred to as:
   a) minorities
   b) culturally different
   c) non-American
   d) white ethnic groups

3. The goal (viewed by Patterson) in practicing counseling or psychotherapy with clients of different cultures is to facilitate the development of:
   a) language communication
   b) client's objectives
   c) self-actualization
   d) nonverbal communication

4. Research methods that examine a hypothesis across cultures are referred to as:
   a) alloplastic research
   b) etic research
   c) emic research
   d) autoplastic research

5. In working with clients of different cultures, counseling "techniques" should:
   a) remain immutable
   b) disregard client's beliefs and values
   c) become flexible
   d) none of the above

6. In cross-cultural counseling, self-actualization is important, but not:
   a) a universal goal
   b) yet developed in counseling techniques
   c) culturally acceptable
   d) a means to social control

7. The goal of psychotherapy is to:
   a) modify external pressures to fit the client's welfare
   b) develop cross-cultural techniques
   c) solve client's dilemmas
   d) change and reorganize a client's adaptive resources

8. A cross-cultural research method that proceeds within a culture is referred to as an:
   a) emic approach
   b) alloplastic approach
   c) autoplastic approach
   d) etic approach

9. Modifying a client's behavior to accommodate external circumstances is referred to as:
   a) socially correct
   b) politically correct
   c) an autoplastic approach
   d) an alloplastic approach

10. Counseling a client to address social conditions as a means of intervention technique is referred to as:
    a) socially correct
    b) politically correct
    c) an autoplastic approach
    d) an alloplastic approach

Case Studies

1. At a rally protesting the lack of black, Hispanic, and Native American professors at a state university campus, students gathered and listened to speakers as they expressed their concerns about inequalities. The rally was part of a week of events creating cultural awareness in higher education. Issues discussed centered around the slow recruitment of minority professors, admissions standards that were biased against minorities, and the lack of ethnic studies on campus.

   The rally had a great turnout. Minority students applauded and cheered as the lectures continued. Nonminority students began gathering at the rally, listening to the many speeches being delivered. A Hispanic male, excited at seeing a large nonminority population attend the rally, commented to a white student, "I'm glad to see you attend the rally. It makes me feel good to see you support our cause." The white student turned and said, "These issues of inequality are important to me. Being Jewish has not always been easy."

2. A Hispanic couple living in California hired a live-in nanny to care for their two daughters. The nanny, a 19-year-old undocumented Hispanic immigrant, came to California to seek employment to earn money and help pay for surgery that her ill father needed. The Hispanic couple were both professionals; the husband was an educator and the wife worked in marketing in the computer industry.

   One day the couple informed the nanny that the family would be relocating to the East Coast in three months. The nanny declined to move with the family, feeling insecure at leaving a large Hispanic population and fearing that the move would bring her in contact with immigration agents at state borders.

Two weeks before leaving, the couple found a job for the nanny working for another family. The nanny was excited about working for another family but expressed that readjusting to another environment was difficult for her. Complicating matters further was the fact that the new family spoke limited Spanish. A month after relocating to the East Coast, the couple received notice from their former nanny that her younger sister had been killed in an auto accident. The nanny was faced with many hardships -- adjusting to a non-bilingual family, not having saved enough money for her father's surgery, and now the loss of her sister. Referral to free counseling services was made; however, she refused on the basis of mistrust and fear of deportation. Two weeks later the nanny suffered a nervous breakdown and was hospitalized.

Classroom Activities

LOCAL RESOURCE PERSONS

Objective

To show the importance of including resource persons from the host culture in training visitors. Resource persons know much about their home culture that is not published in written materials, but it is sometimes difficult for them to respond if asked to "tell about" their own culture.

Procedure

Three exercises are provided to access the resource person's expertise in training situations.

1. A resource person describes a local situation that required a difficult decision, briefing the group for about five minutes on the background for making a decision but *not revealing to the group what decision was actually made.*

Then each member of the group should say what he or she thought the resource person decided to do and why. After each group member has had a chance to guess, the resource person tells what was actually decided and why.

2. Each person in the group makes one statement about the culture represented by the resource person based on the group member's previous experience and then asks the resource person a question about the local culture. After all the members of the group have had a chance to reveal their own experiences with the local culture and ask a question, the resource person describes the attitudes of the group and what the members could do to increase their accuracy of intercultural perception.

3. A resource person stands in front of the group and carries on a conversation with one of the group members. Another person is assigned to stand behind each of the speakers and say aloud what he or she thinks the person is thinking, but not saying, as the two people carry out their conversation.

The observing classroom group then has a picture of both the spoken and unspoken levels of communication in the exchange. The exchange and side comments may be videotaped and the videotape played back to the class later for analysis and discussion.

Insight
Not all cultural similarities and differences are obvious.

THE LABEL EXERCISE

Objective
To show how we often attach labels to people, behave toward them accordingly, and thereby limit our perceptions and restrict communication.

Procedure
Class members choose a variety of labels to categorize people. Some samples are as follows: Tell me I'm right. Flatter me. Ignore me. Criticize me. Treat me as a sex object or Tell me I'm sexy. Interrupt me. Tell me I'm wrong. Treat me as a helpless person with nothing worthwhile to say.

A less risky but almost as effective alternative is to have each label identify a *positive* adjective such as Friendly, Helpful, Sexy, Generous, Loving, etc.

The labels should be typed or printed on self-adhesive stickers (e.g., Avery index stickers) with enough stickers for each participant.

The instructor divides participants into groups of six. The groups are to engage in a discussion on a topic for 10 minutes, at the end of which will be a large group discussion on the topic. During the discussion each member will have a "Label" on his or her forehead for other members to follow. Each member in the small group gets a different label. No one should know what is on his or her own label. All participants should treat the others in the group as though the labels were true. If it would be culturally insensitive to put the label on the forehead, use the person's back where the wearer cannot see his or her own label.

At the end of 10 minutes each participant is to guess what his or her label says. Each member is to convey to the group how he or she felt about how the others were acting toward them. After impressions are checked out and confirmed, then the person may peel off the label and see what it says. When each member has had a chance to see his or her label, they return to a large group for discussion. See how other groups experienced the exercise. How might this situation apply to situations one experiences in real life? Identify words used, nonverbal behaviors, and emotional reactions.

Insight
    All of us are treated by others according to labels they attach to us.

CHAPTER 2

CLIENT, COUNSELOR, AND CONTEXTUAL VARIABLES IN MULTICULTURAL COUNSELING

The second chapter, by Paul B. Pedersen, Mary Fukuyama, and Anne Heath, reviews the research literature about counseling across cultures. The cross-cultural counseling research literature is described from the differing perspectives of the client, counselor, or the environmental context. Each of these different perspectives provides a unique viewpoint in each culture.

Discussion Questions

1. What are the forces that make it necessary for counselors to question their assumptions about counseling as it is applied to different cultures?

2. Compare and contrast the psychological and the anthropological perspectives of cross-cultural issues.

3. Discuss the meaning and impact of "cultural deficit" models.

4. Discuss the reasons Casas gives for why little attention has been given -- until recently -- to minority clients.

5. Discuss the advantages and the disadvantages of a counselor and a client being from the same cultural background.

6. Discuss the importance of Wrenn's term "cultural encapsulation" for counselors.

7. Discuss Sue's dimensions of internal and external control and responsibility as it applies to cross-cultural counseling.

8. How can the training of counselors become more sensitive to cultural issues?

9. Discuss future trends in cross-cultural counseling.

10. Compare and contrast the argument for more cross-cultural emphasis based on "ethical obligations" with the one based on "measured accuracy."

Multiple Choice Questions

1. A cultural approach that assumes that there is a single universal definition of mental health, whatever the person's cultural origin, is referred to as a:
   a) universal definition
   b) comparative framework
   c) worldview approach
   d) multicultural approach

2. An ethnocentric model that promotes the idea that whites are superior to blacks and other nonwhites through biological reasons is called:
   a) autoplastic model
   b) culturally different model
   c) genetic deficiency model
   d) epic approach model

3. Social scientists who describe minorities as disadvantaged because of not being in accordance with middle-class values, language systems, and customs adhere to the:
   a) culturally different model
   b) alloplastic model
   c) cultural deficit model
   d) social view model

4. Treatment that is reformulated to the client's cultural expectations is referred to as:
   a) internal control
   b) cultural grid
   c) Oriental prescription
   d) reformity prescription

5. The perspective that assumes that different groups or individuals have somewhat different definitions of mental health as a result of their unique cultural context best reflects which discipline?
   a) psychology
   b) sociology
   c) social psychology
   d) anthropology

6. A client seeking counseling on the basis of cultural identity is referred to as:
   a) external control
   b) counselor variable
   c) balance as a construct
   d) client variable

7. Disregarding cultural variation among clients and dogmatizing a technique-oriented definition of the counseling process is referred to as:
   a) unethical
   b) cultural bias
   c) counselor encapsulation
   d) none of the above

8. The rubbing of the skin (back, neck, chest areas) with a coin to alleviate a common cold or flu symptoms is called:
   a) voodoo
   b) *curanderismo*
   c) *espiritismo*
   d) *cao gio*

9. A way in which the individual perceives his or her relationship to the world, including other people, institutions, nature, and things, is referred to as:
   a) balance as a construct
   b) comparative framework
   c) worldview
   d) myopic view

10. Asians' perspectives of mental health emphasize the importance of:
    a) self-actualization
    b) balance as a construct
    c) Oriental prescription
    d) a and c

Case Studies

1. A Mexican-American doctoral student interviewing for a graduate assistantship position in a student service program was having a conversation with the director of the retention program. The director discussed the role and responsibility of the assistantship position. The primary responsibility would be outreach targeted specifically toward Hispanic students on campus who were not utilizing the services that were available to them. The director believed that the doctoral student would be a good role model for the Hispanic students and that these students would utilize the services more frequently.

   During the course of the interview the director shared his beliefs as to why students dropped out of college. The director stated that one reason a percentage of students left school was because they do not take advantage of existing support services and another reason was due to biological factors. "Some people are able to learn more and are more intelligent than others," he explained.

2. Susan, a white female at a small liberal arts college, recently ended a three-year relationship with her high school boyfriend. Her roommate Jill noticed that Susan began sleeping in and eating less. Jill believed that this type of behavior was just a phase Susan was going through and that she would soon be herself again.

   One night after returning from a late-night movie, Jill noticed that there was a small container of sleeping pills on Susan's night stand. Jill shared her concerns about the pills with Susan and recommended that Susan seek free counseling available through the campus counseling center. Susan replied that she had thought about counseling but felt uncomfortable because the counselors at the counseling center were all males, and she preferred to meet with a female counselor.

Classroom Activities

PRESENTING MULTICULTURALISM IN SCHOOLS
Designed by Paul B. Pedersen, Syracuse University

Objective

To place the notion of difference in a neutral framework without evaluating those differences in terms of good or bad criteria. We belong to many groups that function in ways similar to cultures and define our individuality in multicultural terms. This exercise was originally used to show primary school children the many groups to which they belong beyond the nationality or ethnic differences that define them as individuals.

Procedure

This exercise works well with a moderate to large group of multiethnic primary or intermediate school children. Their instructors or other school personnel should be present to conduct the exercise and to help interpret its meaning. An average-size school classroom provides sufficient room to accommodate the exercise. Tables and chairs should be moved to one side or to a corner of the room. The exercise may be somewhat noisy. The exercise requires at least 20 minutes to a half hour and should follow a lecture or class discussion about prejudice, discrimination, or problems persons from some cultures have experienced as a result of being different.

A list of neutral characteristics that would be likely to divide the group should be drawn up beforehand in a series of sets. They may include characteristics such as: black shoes/brown shoes/other colored shoes, those wearing red/those not wearing red, those with a penny/those without a penny, and other similarly neutral categories.

1. Students should assemble in a large group in the center of the floor.

2. An instructor reads directions such as: "All those wearing red move to the right side of the room, and all those not wearing red move to the left side of the room." The "team" that assembles first "wins" that set. Then the group reassembles in the center of the floor. Subsequent sets begin with the instructor reading off directions that will divide the group in different ways.

3. After the group has become familiar with the exercise, other differences that are more personal may be used, such as hair color, eye color, tall/short, or other characteristics of the individuals.

4. The more obviously cultural differences such as sex, national background, race, etc., should be saved for the end.

5. A discussion could center around racial/cultural differences being just one of the significant components of our individuality that define us but should not be used to evaluate our worth. The discussion might focus on the role of competition both in the exercise, where the students were on different teams for each set, and in real life, where persons who are different struggle against one another. The students might be encouraged to share incidents of how they have experienced "differentness" in themselves and in others.

Insight

The shifting dynamics of "salience similarity" crosses over differences across cultures.

A CLASSROOM DEBATE
Designed by Anne Pedersen, Syracuse University

Objective

To encourage student involvement in a selected issue.

Procedure

A two-sided topic or question is identified from the chapter or from some application of concepts in the chapter. The class divides into two smaller groups and three members are picked for each side. A week or more should be allowed to prepare for a debate. The debate between the two sides should be organized into a sequence of activities to structure the interaction. It is not necessary to actually believe in the point of view that is being presented, although believing in the issue will no doubt enhance student motivation. *It is important to spend time preparing for the arguments and collecting supporting data to present during the debate.*

An example of a topic for a debate might be the following:

Side One (S1): Cultural differences need more emphasis to define one's culture in *specific* terms that highlight the *separate* identity of each group.

Side Two (S2): Cultural similarities need more emphasis to show how we are *all* bonded together toward *shared* goals and responsibilities irrespective of differences.

The debate may be formatted as follows:

(S1) One side presents opening arguments, with the three members each giving a *three-minute* statement.
(S2) The other side presents opening arguments, with the three members each giving a *three-minute* statement.

(S1) The first side has *three-minutes* for a rebuttal.
(S2) The second side has *three-minutes* for a rebuttal.
(S1) The first side has *three-minutes* for a second rebuttal.
(S2) The second side has *three-minutes* for a second rebuttal.
(S1) The first side has *five-minutes* for a conclusion.
(S2) The second side has *five-minutes* for a conclusion.

Scoring of the debate is done by the rest of the class.

Scoring Criteria: Rate each side on each skill with 1 = low, 10 = high.

I	II		
___	___	1.	analytical skill
___	___	2.	clarity of argument and position
___	___	3.	sophistication of argument
___	___	4.	integration of theory and practice
___	___	5.	relation of argument to reported research
___	___	6.	relation of argument to current events
___	___	7.	effective presentation skills
___	___	8.	general effort involved by the side
___	___	9.	innovative and creative ideas
___	___	10.	ability to work within the stated time limits

Insight
    There are at least two sides to every culturally defined issue.

CHAPTER 3

RACISM IN COUNSELING AS AN ADVERSIVE BEHAVIORAL PROCESS

The third chapter, by Charles R. Ridley, identifies elements of racism as they influence counseling and counselors. Ridley's chapter emphasizes ethnic minority issues and particularly the black/white issues, but the principles of this chapter apply to the full range of relationships between minority and majority cultures.

Discussion Questions

1. What are Ridley's three explanations for why minorities have bad experiences in counseling, and which explanation does he favor?

2. How do you differentiate between racism and prejudice? Provide examples.

3. How might a white counselor unintentionally contribute to racism in counseling?

4. Discuss the importance of the words "behavior" and "systematic" in Ridley's definition of racism.

5. Discuss the difference between overt, covert unintentional, and unintentional racism according to Ridley.

6. Discuss examples of unintentional racism as it relates to cross-cultural counseling.

7. Discuss Ridley's categories of functional and cultural paranoia as they apply to cross-cultural counseling.

8. How might counselors facilitate their own healthy ethnic identity?

9. Discuss Ridley's hypothetical modality profile as a tool to assist cross-cultural counselors.

10. Does Ridley take an optimistic or a pessimistic view of racism in counseling? Support your position with examples.

Multiple Choice Questions

1. Behavior or patterns that systematically tend to deny access to opportunities or privileges to one social group while perpetuating privileges to members of another group is referred to as:
   a) random occurrence
   b) ethnocentrism
   c) systematic privilege
   d) racism

2. A dominant contributing factor to the disproportionate representation of ethnic minorities in pathological diagnostic categories is:
   a) racism
   b) cultural transference
   c) color blindness
   d) pseudotransference

3. An illusion based on the erroneous assumption that all of the client's problems come from being an ethnic minority is called:
   a) stereotyping
   b) prejudice
   c) cultural countertransference
   d) color consciousness

4. An occurrence in which an ethnic minority client responds defensively to racist behaviors by a white therapist is referred to as:
   a) ethnocentrism
   b) cultural ambivalence
   c) pseudotransference
   d) overt racism

5. A client who is able to disclose in any therapy setting, regardless of the therapist's ethnicity, is called:
   a) acculturated
   b) intercultural nonparanoia discloser
   c) functional paranoid
   d) assimilated

6. A clinician's incompetence and inability to differentiate cultural dynamics from pathological dynamics is referred to as:
   a) uncaring
   b) cultural bias
   c) ethnocentrism
   d) misclassification

7. The emotional reaction of a client of one ethnic group transferred to the therapist of a different group is called:
   a) confluent paranoia
   b) cultural countertransference
   c) cultural ambivalence
   d) cultural transference

8. Individual or institutional behavior in which the intentionality is defined by the behavior is referred to as:
   a) prejudice
   b) discrimination
   c) overt racism
   d) covert racism

9. The belief that one's own group is the center of everything and the standard by which all groups are measured is called:
   a) classification
   b) cultural deficit hypothesis
   c) genetic deficiency hypothesis
   d) ethnocentrism

10. The most important assumption for effective treatment with ethnic minority clients is:
    a) cultural congruence
    b) awareness
    c) flexibility of therapeutic techniques
    d) confrontation

Case Studies

1. A Vietnamese high school student was experiencing difficulty in concentrating on her school work because of issues at home. She was hesitant to talk to someone about family issues, but finally she met with her school counselor.

   The Vietnamese student informed the counselor that because of financial hardships her father had started drinking and had become physically violent toward the family. The student also stated that she was staying up late at night comforting her three-year-old sister who was scared and had regressed to wetting her bed.

   The counselor expressed that she was saddened to hear of her situation and conveyed to the student the importance of continuing school so that she could go on to college, graduate, and help contribute at home by helping out financially. The counselor informed the student that her situation was common with recent immigrants and tried to assure her that things would get better.

2. A Chinese American transferring to a four-year university was invited to an orientation for new students. At the orientation the students were given a schedule of spring classes and instructed to tentatively select their classes and then meet with their department advisor for approval.

   After completing the instructions, the Chinese-American student met with his advisor. Wanting to make the student feel welcome, the advisor said to the student at the end of their meeting, "You know, the restaurant across the street sells the best won ton soup around."

Classroom Activities

PERSONAL CULTURAL HISTORY

Objective
　　To become more aware of how our own culture controls our lives by systematically describing our own personal cultural history.

Procedure
　　Class members should complete the following questionnaire:

1. Describe the earliest memory you have of an experience with a person (people) of a cultural or ethnic group different from your own.

2. Who or what has had the most influence in the formation of your attitudes and opinions about people of different cultural groups? In what way?

3. What influences in your experiences have led to the development of positive feelings about your own cultural heritage and background?

4. What influences in your experiences have led to the development of negative feelings, if any, about your own cultural heritage or background?

5. What changes, if any, would you like to make in your own attitudes or experiences in relation to people of other ethnic or cultural groups?

6. Describe an experience in your own life when you feel you were discriminated against for any reason, not necessarily because of your culture.

7. How do you feel _____ should deal with (or not deal with) issues of cultural diversity in American society?

Insight
　　Each of us has a culture.

STEREOTYPES

Objective
　　To create awareness of stereotypic attitudes held toward different groups of people by responses as patterns of similarity across individuals.

Procedure
1. The class or discussion group picks five different ethnic groups. Each person in the group then rates the ethnic groups in conjunction with the statements below. The total score should be added for each ethnic group.

_____Groups_____

A	B	C	D	E	Statements
___	___	___	___	___	not at all aggressive
___	___	___	___	___	conceited about appearance
___	___	___	___	___	very ambitious
___	___	___	___	___	almost always acts as a leader
___	___	___	___	___	very independent
___	___	___	___	___	does not hide emotions at all
___	___	___	___	___	sneaky
___	___	___	___	___	cries easily
___	___	___	___	___	very active
___	___	___	___	___	very logical
___	___	___	___	___	not at all competitive
___	___	___	___	___	feelings easily hurt
___	___	___	___	___	not at all emotional
___	___	___	___	___	very strong need for security
___	___	___	___	___	easily influenced
___	___	___	___	___	very objective
___	___	___	___	___	very self-confident
___	___	___	___	___	easygoing
___	___	___	___	___	has difficulty making decisions
___	___	___	___	___	dependent
___	___	___	___	___	likes math and science very much
___	___	___	___	___	very passive
___	___	___	___	___	very direct
___	___	___	___	___	knows the way of the world
___	___	___	___	___	excitable in a minor crisis
___	___	___	___	___	very adventurous
___	___	___	___	___	very submissive
___	___	___	___	___	hard working, industrious
___	___	___	___	___	not comfortable about being assertive

2. Discuss the following questions:

What similarities in ratings exist? Were there few or many different answers to each item? Are there any sex and age differences noted in the ratings? Why does stereotyping persist? Is it useful? Harmful? What kind of situations tend to stereotype people?

Insight
Stereotypes control our thinking with or without our permission.

THE HIDDEN AGENDA
Designed by Paul B. Pedersen, Syracuse University

Objective
To understand the process of how different cultures manage group situations and pressures by assigning a "hidden group agenda."

Procedure
1. An instructor, knowing the members of the group, designs a list of role tasks that reflect cultural stereotypes relating to the cultural identity of persons in the group. Some of these role tasks might be to always answer in the negative, or always in the positive, or to befriend one other person, or to get into an argument with one other person, or to talk a great deal of the time, or not to talk at all.

2. Each member of the group is given a slip of paper with one role task on it. In 10 minutes the group as a committee must make a decision on an assigned topic. For the 10 minutes, the group discusses the topic, each member performing his or her own role task.

3. No member will be informed of what role task the other members of the group were assigned, and each member will be instructed to keep others from finding out his or her role task.

4. After the 10 minutes are over, the group members can discuss what they thought the other members' role task may have been and how performance of those role tasks affected the committee's activity.

Insight
Our culturally defined "hidden agendas" influence our role in groups.

CHAPTER 4

CROSS-CULTURAL PSYCHOTHERAPY

The fourth chapter, by Julian Wohl, provides an international and cross-disciplinary perspective to the wider field of cross-cultural counseling. Wohl contends that the major barrier to effective cross-cultural psychotherapy lies in the therapist, who must be knowledgeable and competent. The therapist's own biases and stereotypes must be changed before counseling and therapy can be applied to culturally different clients.

Discussion Questions

1. Explain Wohl's statement that "all psychotherapy is cultural; and second, all psychotherapy is cross-cultural."

2. What are the eight most typical cross-cultural psychotherapeutic situations described by Wohl.

3. What are the arguments for and against integrating traditional healing systems from different ethnocultural groups with standard medical practice run on dominant culture assumptions?

4. To what extent can psychotherapy be considered as a cultural universal?

5. What does Wohl mean when he discusses the "special kind of human relationship" associated with psychotherapy?

6. Discuss the Western-developed psychotherapeutic methods practiced by Western or Western-trained individuals with members of other cultures described in Wohl's chapter.

7. Discuss Kinzie's (quoted by Wohl) statement that goals "will be primarily determined by the patient himself and by his culture."

8. In adapting to other cultures is it more important for the therapy or for the therapist to emphasize flexibility?

9. If effectiveness in therapy requires some acceptance of Westernized practice, doesn't this imply that more Western therapy should be applied to non-Western cultures? Discuss.

10. What does Wohl mean when he states that the major barriers to effective cross-cultural psychotherapy lie in the therapists themselves?

Multiple Choice Questions

1. When any component of a psychotherapeutic situation is culturally variant from any other, it is referred to as:
   a) pluralistic
   b) interpersonal
   c) cross-cultural or intercultural
   d) none of the above

2. All psychotherapy that remains in its culture of origin is referred to as:
   a) salient
   b) indigenous or folk
   c) culturally different
   d) Western psychology

3. When a member of one subculture engages in psychotherapy with a patient of another subculture, both of whom are also participants in a larger superordinate culture, it is referred to as:
   a) cultural pluralism
   b) cultural heterogeneity
   c) cross-cultural
   d) culturally different

4. The essence of a psychotherapeutic process is:
   a) cultural understanding
   b) theoretically based
   c) cognitive
   d) human communication

5. The primary medium of psychotherapy is:
   a) technique
   b) verbal
   c) cultural sensitivity
   d) theoretical

6. To improve the therapist's understanding of the patient and to present formulations in a useful manner, Abel (1956) advocated the learning of:
   a) values clarification
   b) languages
   c) cultural facts
   d) cross-cultural techniques

7. In developing a therapeutic relationship with clients of diverse cultures, the therapist should assess the:
   a) client's presenting problem
   b) client's expectation of therapy and therapist
   c) level of English proficiency
   d) a and b

8. A specially created professional situation in which a recognized, qualified expert and a client who needs help have agreed formally to meet on a regular basis to reduce psychological distress is called:
   a) consulting
   b) psychotherapy
   c) clinical assessment
   d) a and c

9. Bustamente (1957) referred to clients of other cultures who participated in tradition as:
   a) cross-cultural
   b) pluralistic
   c) polycultural
   d) monocultural

10. A cultural transplant of Western psychotherapy to non-Western society may be considered as:
    a) effective cross-cultural psychotherapy
    b) universally accepted
    c) nontransferable
    d) none of the above

Case Studies

1. A Taiwanese student returned to her home country after receiving her graduate degree in counseling in the United States. Her initial work consisted of explaining the counseling process and how counseling was used in the United States. Many of her contacts could not believe that Americans would tell their personal stories to a stranger and that the stranger was paid to listen.

After a short time in Taiwan, the student returned to the United States hoping to work as a counselor at a university. She explained that it was difficult to do counseling in a culture that did not believe in discussing personal or family matters outside the home.

2. A 50-year-old Mexican woman went to her physician because of chest pains. After an examination and a conversation with the patient, the physician related the woman's pains to stress due to not attending her mother's funeral. The physician referred the woman to a counselor. The counselor, a Mexican American, learned that the woman had not received notice of her mother's death until months later because her family in Mexico had no phone.

The counselor assessed that her pain was caused by the guilt that she carried. The counselor also learned that the woman had no family or relatives nearby. To address her needs, the counselor contacted a local parish that had mass in Spanish. He spoke with the priest and informed him of the situation. The priest was able to meet with the woman that afternoon.

A few weeks later the Mexican woman contacted the counselor and thanked him for his help. The woman said that the priest was able to have a rosary and a mass for her mother.

Classroom Activities

ROLE-PLAYING A PROBLEM IN A GROUP

Objective
　　To allow a group an opportunity to project themselves into a cross-cultural problem, rather than discussion of a problem, by assuming roles of persons involved in that problem, not necessarily their own culture roles. A problem-solving format is needed to get at an ambiguous problem or crisis area in the group's discussion, especially when the group is divided on an issue and unable to come to a resolution.

Procedure
1. Members of the group select roles in which they will participate in a group role-play situation to work on a cross-cultural problem, which may be from their own culture or a contrasting culture. A problem may have already emerged in group discussion.

2. One or more members should remain in the role of an observer or referee to facilitate debriefing.

3. The members act out in their assumed roles the conflict situation of the selected problem.

4. After role-playing, members tell the group what they learned about the problem.

Insight
　　Multicultural problems are not obstructions when they belong to yourself.

WORLD PICTURE TEST
Developed by Paul B. Pedersen, Syracuse University

Objective
　　To clarify participants' understanding of countries and cultures of the world through their knowledge of geography.

Procedure
1. Each participant uses a sheet of paper and a pen to:
　　a. draw a map of the world as best as he or she can within a five-minute time
　　　 period,
　　b. name as many of the countries as possible,
　　c. mark any country he or she has visited for a week or longer.

2. The participants exchange papers with another member of the group and discuss what differences are evidenced in what the other person put into his or her drawing and/or left out of the drawing.

3. The following points are then discussed:

3. The following points are then discussed:
    a. Does a person's awareness of the shape of a country reveal that person's awareness of the culture?
    b. When a person leaves out a country, what does that mean?
    c. When a person leaves out a continent, what does that mean?
    d. What country did the person place in the center of the map and what does that mean?
    e. When a person draws a country out of place in relation to other countries, what does that mean?
    f. Were the participants better acquainted with countries they had visited?
    g. When a person objects violently to doing the drawing, what does that mean?
    h. How well did the participants draw home countries of other group members?
    i. What do the participants plan to do as a result of what they learned in this exercise?

Insight

   The more familiar you are with a country, the more accurate your picture of that country is likely to be.

CHAPTER 5

ETHICS IN MULTICULTURAL COUNSELING

The fifth chapter, by Teresa D. LaFromboise and Sandra L. Foster, provides the best review to date of ethical issues related to cross-cultural counseling. Although professional associations for counselors and therapists have determined that counseling and therapy must be provided in culturally appropriate ways, the profession has not gone beyond rhetorical support of these principles. LaFromboise and Foster provide the documentation for an informed discussion of the ethical issues.

Discussion Questions

1. What is the "ethical crisis in cross-cultural counseling practice"?

2. What is the argument against including the perspectives of "women, ethnic/racial minority persons, poor persons, and old people" as special interest groups in the APA ethical guidelines?

3. To what extent are the ethical guidelines designed to protect the profession and to what extent are they intended to protect the client?

4. What are some of the areas of cross-cultural counseling where ethical issues might arise? Give examples.

5. Why is there not more emphasis on cross-cultural counseling in the training of counselors and therapists?

6. How would you like to see cross-cultural topics integrated into the training of counselors? Defend your plan.

7. What do LaFromboise and Foster mean when they describe an "ethic of caring and responsibility" as "a promising dialectic that could be considered in resolving ethical dilemmas across cultures"?

8. Distinguish between what Gilligan describes as a "care perspective" and a "justice perspective" in multicultural ethical decision making.

9. What does Ivey mean in suggesting that we move toward a more relational view of ethics?

10. What is the role of a field component in training multicultural counselors about ethics?

Multiple Choice Questions

1. APA Principles reflect the prevailing individualistic orientation based on:
   a) pluralistic values
   b) minority cultural values
   c) majority cultural values
   d) none of the above

2. Casas (1986) stated that counseling interventions are based only on normative data of:
   a) cultural groups
   b) lower socioeconomic class
   c) white middle class
   d) a and b

3. Zuniga defines American psychological training as:
   a) culturally sensitive
   b) Euro-American based
   c) technique based
   d) ethnocentric and negligent

4. According to Triandis (1976), differences that are perceived as beneficial to society as a whole are referred to as:
   a) altruism
   b) collectivism
   c) positive multiculturalism
   d) none of the above

5. LaFromboise (1988) illustrated that the psychology service provided for Native American Indians compared with that for the general population was:
   a) 1 to 8,000
   b) 1 to 2,000
   c) untrained
   d) nonminority

6. A profession that is composed of socioculturally diverse members representing the composition of a society is called:
   a) status quo
   b) affirmative action
   c) demographic parity
   d) equality

7. Text materials on cultural manifestations of morality for multicultural ethics training are:
   a) accepted guidelines
   b) culturally biased
   c) limited
   d) none of the above

8. According to Pedersen (1986), the Ethical Principles are:
   a) acceptable
   b) culturally sensitive
   c) culturally encapsulated
   d) a and b

9. Ethical issues in counseling involve:
   a) cultural knowledge and training
   b) cultural biases
   c) cultural misunderstanding
   d) all of the above

10. The commitment to personal liberty, the ideal of autonomy, and use of a social contract model is called:
   a) self-actualization
   b) justice perspective
   c) care perspective
   d) all of the above

Case Studies

1. A Chinese graduate student recently finished his master's degree in counseling psychology and was preparing to apply to a doctoral program. The student received acceptances from numerous universities throughout the country. In addition, the student was offered fellowships from several prestigious universities.

The Chinese student visited the doctoral programs at universities that were within reasonable driving distance. From universities that were out of state, the student received information through the mail.

After narrowing the selection to five universities, the student met with his advisor to decide on which school to attend. After a lengthy conversation with his advisor the student finally made a decision. One important factor that he had overlooked was the fact that none of the five schools had faculty of color, specifically professors of Chinese descent.

2. Maria, a 17-year-old first-generation Mexican-American high school student, was angry and upset because she was not given permission to attend a field trip to visit a local university. Maria's friends were concerned about her behavior and informed a counselor at the Counseling and Guidance Center. The counselor, a female Mexican American, met with Maria to find out what was troubling her. Maria explained that she would like to attend college but that her family did not support her decision. Maria mentioned that her father wanted her to stay home and help her mother around the house, and that maybe in a few years when she was older she could possibly go on to school. Maria believed her father's real reason for not supporting her in continuing her education was because of the rapes that were occurring on college campuses.

The counselor, Ms. Bustamante, shared with Maria that she too was not supported by her parents when she went to college. But Ms. Bustamante was not angry at her parents, because she knew that her parents really loved her. Instead, she found a way to convey to her parents the benefits of attending college.

Ms. Bustamante advised Maria to do the same and suggested that she share with her parents information about different colleges. In addition, Ms. Bustamante suggested that Maria gather information about housing and, if possible, the security services the campuses offer students.

Classroom Activities

STEREOTYPES

Objective

To define stereotypes and become more aware of where we find them and how they are reinforced (e.g., by the media). Stereotypes are generalizations based on some fact, attributes, or categories and labels.

Procedure
1. Group members should complete the following statements on a separate sheet of paper. Group members can answer according to their own personal opinions or according to what they think "everybody knows" about the particular groups mentioned.

    a. Almost everyone agrees that intelligent, educated, assertive American women today are_____
    b. Some consistent, personal characteristics of people over the age of 65 are _____
    c. It is common knowledge that Blacks raised in the ghetto are _____
    d. Some of the problems with Asian Americans are _____
    e. (True or False) Almost everyone belonging to a minority group agrees that most middle class whites are racist.

2. After the statements are completed, the papers should be handed in to a facilitator or instructor.

3. Several volunteers should read the answers to each statement above. Also, one volunteer for each statement should take notes on the answers and be ready to facilitate a discussion later.

4. Each statement below should then be discussed for about 15 minutes beginning with the volunteer who took notes. The focus should be on key words in each statement and on questions dealing with where the students got the answers. How does the media influence the development and maintenance of stereotypes?
    a. Assertive women are often confused with being masculine, aggressive, and "women's libbers."
    b. Just what do we mean by consistent, personal characteristics? Do older people begin to act in certain ways because we expect them to?
    c. How many people are familiar enough with a black ghetto to have an idea of what life is like there? Where does the word "ghetto" come from? What do we mean by ghetto? How does the media influence our "expectations" that blacks and ghettos go hand in hand?

d. How do we define Asian Americans? What are some of the problems that Asians themselves identify as being part of a minority in the United States? Who has the problem?
   e. What is a middle-class white? How do we define the word racist?

Insight

There is more than one legitimate approach to education across cultures.

THE CULTURAL PERSPECTIVES OF EDUCATION IN SOCIETY
Adapted and modified from *Dynamics of Groups at Work*, Herbert A. Thelen (University of Chicago, 1956), by permission

Objective

To contrast two divergent and alternative perspectives for viewing education that highlight differences in educational values in a multicultural educational environment.

Procedure

The following directions should be read to the group: In multicultural education generally, it seems to me that we are in the middle of an argument. Our problem is to restate the argument in such a way that we can settle it. We are ready to try to understand what we know about learning wherever it occurs and to see what the implications are for classroom situations. The simplest expression of the argument is through a sampling of the value conflicts it contains in two cultural perspectives.

Perspective A: I want my child to be treated as an *individual* by teachers who *center* their attention on the *children* and see themselves essentially as *guides*. Children are capable of *planning* and *discussing* their experiences, of being *guided from within*. The important thing is understanding and *insight* that leads to *growth*. I want them through firsthand experience to learn the meaning of *freedom*, to understand and be committed to a *democratic* way of life. But, above all, I want them to be adequate people, with a rich and ennobling *subjective inner life*; only thus can they achieve the creative *spontaneity* that is humanity's most precious attribute.

Perspective B: The teachers are instruments of *society* and are hired primarily because of their mastery of disciplines arranged in *school subjects*. Their job is to give *instruction* and to communicate not single interesting facts but rather ideas organized in meaningful relationship to each other, as in a *lecture*. Teachers know the material to be covered, and it is their responsibility *to plan* in such a way that it will be covered. Teachers know that getting ahead in this world requires ability to meet the *demands of the community*, and that only through *drill and practice* can school *achievement* become part of one's habit pattern. Many of the important things in life were discovered by others and are learned through *vicarious experience dominated* by these great *authorities*. The child is free to think as he or she wishes, but in the objective world of action he or she must *conform* to the standard of the community.

Each group member is to circle the number in the following semantic differential that describes his or her own commitment to basic aims of education in society.

Individual	1	2	3	4	5	6	7	Society
Child-centered	1	2	3	4	5	6	7	Subject-centered
Guidance	1	2	3	4	5	6	7	Instruction
Discussion	1	2	3	4	5	6	7	Lecture
Pupil planning	1	2	3	4	5	6	7	Teacher planning
Intrinsic motivation	1	2	3	4	5	6	7	Extrinsic motivation
Insight learning	1	2	3	4	5	6	7	Drill and practice
Growth	1	2	3	4	5	6	7	Achievement
Firsthand experience	1	2	3	4	5	6	7	Vicarious experience
Freedom	1	2	3	4	5	6	7	Dominance
Democratic	1	2	3	4	5	6	7	Authoritarian
Subjective world	1	2	3	4	5	6	7	Objective world
Spontaneity	1	2	3	4	5	6	7	Conformity

Insight

There is more than one way to look at the ideal educational process.

CHAPTER 6

A MODEL FOR COUNSELING ASIAN AMERICANS

The sixth chapter, by Harry H. L. Kitano, reviews the ways that a Japanese American might approach counseling. Kitano demonstrates how both the Japanese and the American stereotypes are combined in the Japanese-American situation. This chapter points out the dangers of stereotyping and demonstrates clearly that culture is complex and dynamic.

Discussion Questions

1. What does Kitano mean in describing Asian Americans as an "invisible group"?

2. Why do so many Asian Americans remain outside the mainstream "American" norms according to Kitano and the persons he cites?

3. What are some problems that arise in developing a model of counseling specifically for Asian Americans?

4. Explain Kitano's model juxtaposing high/low assimilation with high/low ethnic identity.

5. What guidelines would you identify as most important for yourself as you work with Asian-American clients?

6. Describe an example of "culture conflict" that incorporates at least two of Kitano's categories in a family setting.

7. What is the likelihood of concepts popular among Asian and Asian-American cultures also being found useful for other cultural groups? What concepts would you recommend?

8. What does Kitano mean when he describes Asians as coming from cultures that are not primarily psychologically oriented?

9. What are the positive and negative characteristics of a client who is Type B, "high assimilation, high ethnic identity," according to Kitano?

10. How has the "new immigration" changed the Asian-American community in recent years? Use Kitano's model of ethnic identity and assimilation to answer this question.

Multiple Choice Questions

1. Two variables that appear most critical when dealing with Asian Americans are:
   a) immigration/naturalization
   b) religion/politics
   c) assimilation/ethnic identity
   d) none of the above

2. The lessening of ethnic identity with length of time in America is referred to as:
   a) melting pot
   b) integration
   c) pluralism
   d) straight line theory

3. In the straight line theory, Type C is associated with:
   a) high assimilation/low ethnic identity
   b) high assimilation/high ethnic identity
   c) high ethnic identity/low assimilation
   d) low ethnic identity/low assimilation

4. An individual whose cultural commitment is via ethnic foods, ethnic movies, or ethnic festivals in lieu of learning language or history is referred to as:
   a) high assimilation/low ethnic identity
   b) a wanna be
   c) mainstreaming
   d) symbolic ethnicity

5. An individual who feels comfortable and knowledgeable about both cultures, has friends in each, and belongs to organizations spanning the cultures is called:
   a) cross-cultural
   b) high ethnic identity/low assimilation
   c) multicultural
   d) bicultural

6. Using the straight line model, therapeutic techniques that are verbally oriented work least with:
   a) Type A
   b) Type B
   c) Type C
   d) Type D

7. In the straight line model assessing a conflict within families in which often parents are in one category and the children in another is referred to as:
   a) bicultural stress
   b) assimilation stress
   c) acculturation conflict
   d) culture conflict

8. Sue and Zane (1986) defined the assignment of a nonethnic counselor of inappropriate sex or age to work with traditional Asians as:
   a) lack of achieved credibility
   b) nonempathetic understanding
   c) lack of ascribed credibility
   d) a and b

9. A Japanese therapeutic process that focuses on the important influences in the client's life, especially the mother, is referred to as:
   a) Morita therapy
   b) Ajase complex therapy
   c) Naikan therapy
   d) Okonogi contrast

10. The retention of customs, attitudes, and beliefs of cultural origin is referred to as:
    a) ethnic identity
    b) culturally different
    c) amalgamation
    d) none of the above

Case Studies

1. A counselor at an urban high school was leaving his office after school to meet with a teacher in another building. As he approached the school library he heard two people screaming and shouting. As the counselor went to see what the commotion was about, he witnessed a Vietnamese woman hitting a young Vietnamese female with an umbrella. The counselor immediately stopped the woman from hitting the student and escorted them to the administration office.

   Mrs. Troung, a volunteer teacher's aide, was called in to assist with the matter. After a long discussion with the two Vietnamese women, Mrs. Troung shared with the counselor the following: The older Vietnamese woman was the mother of the student. She was upset because the daughter had told the mother that she had been studying at the school library and that was why she had arrived home late for the past several nights. The mother had come to the school that day to make sure her daughter was really studying. Upon arriving at the school, the mother found her daughter holding hands with a Vietnamese boy. The mother began hitting her daughter for lying. The parent's rule was that she was not to have a boyfriend until she was ready to marry.

2. An Asian family met with a family therapist because the parents were having difficulty controlling their oldest son. The parents were immigrants and were referred to family services via a community agency. The therapist, a Hispanic female, experienced difficulty in establishing a smooth session. Although she was aware of the cultural factors in counseling Asian families, she realized that for some reason the session had not gone as well as she wanted.

   As the session came to an end the therapist scheduled an appointment for the family for the following week. A couple of days later the family cancelled their appointment and asked if they could have a referral. The therapist asked if she had upset them in any way and the mother responded that she had not; however, she did comment that her husband would feel more comfortable if the therapist were an older Asian male.

Classroom Activities

NO QUESTIONS ASKED
Developed by Paul B. Pedersen, Syracuse University

Objective
    To enable participants to abandon their previously learned categories of relevance, and see all of the surroundings as possibly offering clues to the nature of the Asian-American community in which they find themselves.

Procedure

This exercise is designed to be "free-form" and is therefore difficult to control; thus it requires the facilitator or instructor to have a good knowledge of the Asian-American community and be alert to any errors in observation.

1. Participants should go into the community for at least one afternoon with instructions to learn as much about it as possible without asking direct questions -- preferably without asking questions at all.

2. Afterward, in group discussions, the facilitator or instructor asks specific questions about the community.

Insight

Much can be learned in another culture by watching and listening without asking questions.

ROLE-PLAYING A NEWSPAPER INCIDENT
Developed by Paul B. Pedersen, Syracuse University

Objective

To demonstrate how persons from different backgrounds view differently everyday events that involve persons from more than one culture.

Procedure

1. The instructor distributes one or more newspapers to the group and asks the members to examine the papers.

2. Group members each select from the paper a story involving Asian Americans with which they can identify and that could possibly have happened to them personally.

3. Each member of the group projects himself or herself into the role of one main person in the selected story and tells the group about what happened as though it had happened to him or her personally. Group members are free to ask questions of the person telling the story to explicate aspects of the story that they find difficult to understand.

Insight

Learning about multiculturalism will encourage students to read the newspapers with greater insight.

CHAPTER 7

COUNSELING THE HISPANIC CLIENT: A THEORETICAL AND APPLIED PERSPECTIVE

The seventh chapter, by J. Manuel Casas and Melba J. T. Vasquez, documents the importance of bilingual and bicultural approaches to counseling, with special reference to Hispanic people. The rapid growth of the Hispanic population relative to the total U.S. population indicates a considerable need to know more about models that work in the Hispanic setting. This chapter also points out how broadly defined the "Hispanic" label is when applied to Spanish-speaking populations.

Discussion Questions

1. What are some of the changes you expect to occur as a result of minority groups, such as the Hispanics, growing more rapidly than whites and what are the implications of those changes for counseling?

2. Explain how you would use the framework for counseling the Hispanic client presented by Casas and Vasquez.

3. Discuss the danger of assuming a universal measure of normality.

4. In what specific ways does the assumed "superior" evaluation of individualism demonstrate itself in counseling practice?

5. Discuss the implications of acculturation for counseling the Hispanic client.

6. What are the strengths and weaknesses of identifying a particular approach for counseling Hispanics as compared to a more generalized sensitivity to cultural differences?

7. What do Casas and Vasquez mean when they propose the incorporation of preventive and developmental interventions?

8. Give examples of counselor variables (professional and personal attitudes and beliefs) that relate to cross-cultural counseling effectiveness?

9. Give examples of client variables (individual, sociocultural, sociohistorical, and environmental) that relate to cross-cultural counseling effectiveness.

10. Give examples of counseling process variables (counseling approaches, use or misuse of theory, and environmental milieu) that relate to cross-cultural counseling effectiveness.

Multiple Choice Questions

1. According to Casas and Vasquez (1989), what two Hispanic groups maintain high fertility rates:
   a) Colombians/Cubans
   b) Peruvians/Venezuelans
   c) Puerto Ricans/Mexican Americans
   d) Cubans/Chicanos

2. A myriad of topics concerning Hispanics fall into three broad categories. The largest amount of published work on Hispanics focuses on what variable:
   a) counselor variable
   b) counseling process
   c) client variable
   d) a and b

3. In traditional Hispanic culture, a value that is of high priority is:
   a) education
   b) family
   c) independence
   d) religion

4. An element that contributes to the dynamic, ever-changing aspect of the Hispanic population is:
   a) language
   b) religion
   c) acculturation
   d) immigration

5. According to Casas and Vasquez, Hispanics attribute control to:
   a) internal locus
   b) external locus
   c) self-control
   d) a and b

6. Ivey, Ivey, and Simek-Downing (1986) considered a counselor "who has the capacity to understand many individuals who are vastly different from the counselor and who also has the ability to generate a maximum number of thoughts, words, and behaviors to communicate with a variety of diverse groups inside and outside the counselor's culture" to have:
   a) cultural knowledge
   b) pluralistic ideology
   c) cultural respect
   d) cultural empathy

7. A theoretical counseling approach appropriate for many ethnic minorities, including Mexican Americans, that includes environmental focus and skill building and does not blame the victims is referred to as:
   a) psychodynamic approach
   b) Gestalt approach
   c) humanistic approach
   d) behavioral approach

8. A counseling approach that attends to behavior, affect, sensations, images, cognitions, interpersonal relations, and biological functions is known as:
   a) multicultural counseling
   b) pluralistic approach
   c) cognitive approach
   d) multimodal approach

9. Interventions that may be defined as those that "present or forestall onset of problems or needs through anticipation of the consequence of non-action" are referred to as:
   a) developmental interventions
   b) crisis interventions
   c) preventive interventions
   d) post interventions

10. Time orientation that Hispanics often display is:
    a) present time orientation
    b) past time orientation
    c) future time orientation
    d) none of the above

Case Studies

1. Jessica, a 22-year-old Mexican-American female from central Illinois, left home to attend college in California. A few weeks into the semester, she began to notice the cultural difference between her and other Hispanics on campus. Jessica noticed that the majority of the Hispanics were able to speak both English and Spanish fluently. Although her parents spoke Spanish at home, it was not mandatory that the children be bilingual.

   In her English class, of predominantly white students, Jessica felt comfortable and relaxed. However, in a Chicano studies course that fulfilled the cultural pluralism requirement for graduation, she felt out of place because she did not share the same types of experiences as other Hispanics in the class.

   Jessica shared her feelings with the Chicano studies professor, who was very sensitive to the issue. The professor responded by telling Jessica that not all Mexican Americans share the same sociocultural experience and that people need to understand and respect the values of others.

2. Raquel, a 29-year-old Hispanic college student, recently received her bachelor of arts degree in English. Raquel graduated with honors and was the first of seven siblings to finish college. Raquel was married and had two children, ages two and four. Her husband worked the swing shift at a supermarket, and she worked as a teacher's aide at an elementary school. During the day Raquel's husband took care of the children and in the afternoon he left them with his mother. Raquel attended classes three nights a week and after class she picked up the children.

   Two weeks before graduation Raquel was informed about her nomination for an award by the faculty in her department. The award recognized outstanding students in comparative English literature. In addition, the department chairperson met with Raquel to discuss graduate school. Raquel was offered a scholarship to attend the master's program in English the following fall.

   Raquel was torn between graduate school and staying at home with her children. After several days of thinking about the offer, she decided that she would take a year off from school so that she could be with her family. Coincidentally, Raquel did not receive the award for which she had been nominated.

Classroom Activities

A FREE DRAWING TEST

Objective

To produce data on differential subconscious response to culture-loaded concepts by using a free drawing test.

Procedure

1. Group members select a number of concepts (nouns, verbs, etc.) that seem to be clearly related to the cultures of the group.

2. Each member draws an X in the middle of a blank sheet of paper.

3. Each member places his or her pencil on the center of the X and begins drawing when the instructor or a member of the group mentions one of the previously selected concepts. The members should not be given any guidance on what to draw but merely told to form one continuous line in any direction or shape as they are motivated by the announced concept.

4. A scoring technique should be applied by the instructor to compare the drawings, by assigning values as to whether the drawing is open, closed, large, small, complex, simple, requiring more time, requiring less time, angular, rounded, number of directional changes, number of reversals, recognizable picture, begins with an upstroke, begins with a downstroke, ends with an upstroke, ends with a downstroke, and so on. Other criteria to compare the drawings may be suggested by the group, growing out of apparent similarities and differences.

5. The group then discusses whether similarities and differences in the drawings seem to coincide with cultural differences in the group in terms of the covert effects culture has on behavior.

Insight

Not all of our culturally learned patterns are completely conscious.

CROSS-CULTURAL TRAINING EXERCISE FOR INTERPRETING POLICY
Designed by Paul B. Pedersen, Syracuse University

Objective

To determine culture-specific patterns of common and variant interpretations, as well as level of comprehension of written material containing word deletions.

Procedure

1. The instructor selects one or more paragraphs drawn from institutional rhetoric involving cross-cultural values.

2. The instructor then omits at least 10 or 15 words, keeping the space where these words were extracted blank for the participants to write in their own words as they consider appropriate.

3. Each participant is given a copy of the prepared paragraph and a pencil.

4. After filling in the blanks to give the paragraph meaning, members of the group compare their interpretations and discuss them according to culture-specific variables.

Example:
"The Board of Regents has _____ itself and the University of Minnesota to the policy that there shall be no _____ in the treatment of_____ _____ because of _____. This is a guiding policy in the _____ _____ of students in all colleges and in their _____ _____. It is also to be a governing principle in University-owned and University-approved housing, in food services, student unions, extra-curricular activities and all other student and staff services. This policy must also be _____ in the _____ _____ of students either by the University or by _____ through the University and in the _____ of faculty and civil service staff." *

Insight
    Policy statements contain many cultural assumptions.

---
* Statement on Human Rights, University of Minnesota 1971-1972 Bulletin on General Information.

CHAPTER 8

PROVIDING COUNSELING SERVICES FOR NATIVE AMERICAN INDIANS: CLIENT, COUNSELOR, AND COMMUNITY CHARACTERISTICS

The eighth chapter, by Joseph E. Trimble and Candace M. Fleming, reviews literature describing the American Indian client. The great diversity within the American Indian nations is often overlooked in stereotyped treatments of "Indians." This chapter points out the importance of both within-group differences and between-group differences when working with American Indian clients.

Discussion Questions

1. What are the negative consequences of describing Native American Indians in a collective manner that de-emphasizes diversity?

2. What are the political dynamics likely to influence the effectiveness of cross-cultural counseling more with Native American Indians than with any of the other minority groups?

3. What are some of the reasons that Native American Indians underutilize mental health services?

4. Why do Trimble and Fleming consider trust and flexibility among the most important counselor characteristics for working with Native American Indians?

5. Describe the generalized system of values that is said to characterize Native American Indians.

6. Discuss the adequacy of Bryde's six important characteristics for counselors of Native American Indians.

7. Describe and discuss your treatment plan for working with "Mary" as described in this chapter.

8. Describe and discuss your treatment plan for working with "Terry" as described in this chapter.

9. Describe and discuss your treatment plan for working with "Joanne" as described in this chapter.

10. Describe how you would assess a client's "acculturative status" in counseling.

Multiple Choice Questions

1. Two important characteristics needed when counseling Native American clients are:
   a) language and religion
   b) historical and social understanding
   c) empathy and warmth
   d) trust and flexibility

2. Research has suggested that a client variable in working with Native Americans is:
   a) self-disclosure
   b) client/counselor ethnic match
   c) future time orientation
   d) none of the above

3. Many traditional Native American Indians place an importance on:
   a) "living with" the environment
   b) self-actualization
   c) individuality
   d) b and c

4. A counseling style that Native American Indian students feel comfortable with is:
   a) psychodynamic approach
   b) directive approach
   c) Rogerian approach
   d) humanistic approach

5. Within the Native American Indian culture, a component of high value is:
   a) self-disclosure
   b) family
   c) time orientation
   d) a and c

6. Family patterns, peer group relationships, and community relationships are referred to as:
   a) client variables
   b) counselor variables
   c) ecological processes
   d) none of the above

7. A process in which *some* Native Americans have learned to cope with emotional and stressful conditions in a culturally unique way is referred to as:
   a) indigenous psychotherapy
   b) sweat house
   c) *wacinko*
   d) a and c

8. A federal agency that determines if Native Americans are entitled to government services is:
   a) National Tribal Chairman's Association
   b) Department of Education
   c) Bureau of Census
   d) Bureau of Indian Affairs

9. "Breeds" or people of mixed marriages are not considered:
   a) multicultural
   b) cross-cultural
   c) pluralistic
   d) ethnically pure

10. Counselors working with Native Americans out of community mental health centers are quick to point out that Native Americans:
   a) underutilize services
   b) have a higher termination ratio
   c) respond to treatment less
   d) all of the above

Case Studies

1. Leonard, a Lakota Indian, returned home to the reservation after serving three years in the armed services. During Leonard's stay in the marines he was stationed at several bases in the United States and was sent to Germany for a year. At a sweat lodge, after his return, many of Leonard's friends and older members of the tribe shared stories of their ancestors. When Leonard was a child he remembered listening to his father tell stories about his great-grandfather, and he had always enjoyed learning about his family history. However, Leonard noticed that now these stories did not mean anything to him and that he could not understand the importance that his tribe placed on talking about individuals who no longer existed.

Several weeks after his return home from the service, Leonard found himself in conflict with his parents and siblings. Many of his friends claimed that Leonard was acting as though he was too good to be a Lakota Indian. The conflict between family and friends caused Leonard much pain. He felt that no one understood him. He felt alone. Leonard wanted to leave the reservation to find work so that he could save his money and travel through Europe; however, he knew that with only a high school education getting a job would be difficult.

Leonard became more depressed about the conflict that he was experiencing at home. He realized he could no longer live on the reservation and be happy. After two months at home, Leonard left the reservation and reenlisted in the marines for another full term.

2. In *The Silent Language* (Doubleday, 1959), Edward T. Hall talked about his experience working for a soil conservation program at a Navajo reservation. While supervising construction of small earth dams, he noticed that the Navajo workmen operated in a relaxed pace as though they had no worries at all. He recalled sharing his American values about the hard work ethic and that working hard today will bring rewards tomorrow. Hall noticed that this did not bring about changes in their work behavior.

After discussing this problem with a friend who had spent all his life on a reservation, Hall decided to approach the Navajo workmen in a different manner. He recalled talking with the work crew and telling them how the "American government was giving them money to get out of debt by providing them jobs near their families, and giving them water for their sheep." Hall stressed the fact that in return they had to work hard for eight hours a day. He noticed that the change in approach altered their work performance.

Classroom Activities

CULTURAL VALUE SYSTEMS WITH CONFLICTING POINTS OF VIEW
Developed by Paul B. Pedersen, Syracuse University

Objective

To demonstrate contrasting and conflicting aspects of interactions between persons who do not share the same basic assumptions by discussing value conflicts.

Procedure

1. The group divides into two or more individual or group units. One or more observers are assigned to take notes and referee.

2. The groups generate alternative value systems from the members' own backgrounds (Example: a system that is property- or rule-oriented and one that is person-oriented).

3. Each value system is assigned to one of the individual or group units.

4. A topic is discussed in which those value systems are likely to be contrasting or conflicting with one another.

5. Each individual or group unit must maintain a position consistent with the assigned value system.

6. Each individual or group is evaluated according to:

    a. whether they maintained a position consistent with their assigned value system,

    b. whether they were more skillful in developing a powerful argument for their position based on these borrowed values.

Insight

Cultures are not always in agreement on important issues.

CULTURAL IMPACT STORYTELLING

Objective

To stimulate new perceptions and development of new knowledge through storytelling. The American Indians, along with many other ethnic groups, used storytelling as a major vehicle in disseminating their culture. Such an activity is what stimulated Alex Haley to trace his "roots." Many cultures fell away from the art of storytelling with the advent of mass-produced printed communication. Storytelling, however, assists us to get in touch quite vividly with our personal "stories" and thus to know more of ourselves. From Paulo Freire in *Pedagogy of the Oppressed* (Continuum, 1970).

Procedure

As the participants perform the exercise they should think specifically of those people or events that, from a cultural perspective, have significantly affected them.

1. Using large sheets of paper and crayons, the participants should graphically (i.e., using symbols, sketches, etc.) represent the events, the joys, the sorrows, the people, and the decisions that have had an effect on the unique cultural development of each of them.

2. Then, looking over the graphic, each participant should place a plus (+) sign by one event he or she considers a highly positive experience. Next a negative (-) sign should be placed by one event each participant believes to be an extremely negative experience.

3. Each participant then hangs the graphic before the group where all can see and tells his or her story. The "+" and "-" experiences should be described in detail.

4. Variables that were operative, creating either a positive or a negative impact, should be analyzed. Can the variables be explained with a concept or a theory?

Insight

Much of our thinking process is guided by culturally learned stories.

CHAPTER 9

COUNSELING FOREIGN STUDENTS

The ninth chapter, by Kay Thomas and Gary Althen, provides some practical guidelines for working with international students. International students demonstrate an "artificial" cultural group where the only thing they all have in common is their "foreign" or "alien" background in the host country. The complex variety presented by international students from different countries provides a rich texture of backgrounds to the counselor.

Discussion Questions

1. What are the differences in accommodation experienced by foreign students as compared with ethnic minorities, refugees, or immigrants?

2. How would Kluckhohn and Strodtbeck's (1961) five dimensions of cultural variation help counselors adapt counseling to different foreign students?

3. Which of the 14 different adjustment problems mentioned in this chapter do you consider to be most troublesome for foreign students and why?

4. Why is it important to distinguish between problems foreign students have and the problems they are likely to bring to counseling?

5. Why is cultural adjustment a psychosocial process?

6. What do we know from the research literature about culture shock and how does that literature apply to foreign students?

7. What symptoms would indicate that cultural adjustment was becoming a problem for a foreign student?

8. How might a foreign student present a different set of symptoms to the counselor than other nonforeign student clients?

9. How might a counselor modify counseling style when working with foreign students according to the literature?

10. Compare and contrast cognitive therapy with behavioral therapy in working with foreign students.

Multiple Choice Questions

1. Members of collective-oriented society see themselves as:
   a) individualistic
   b) narcissistic
   c) groups, families, tribes
   d) a and b

2. Behavior that is culturally prescribed is referred to as:
   a) normal
   b) high-context culture
   c) low-context culture
   d) b and c

3. The focus on how an individual integrates into the social interaction of a new culture is referred to as:
   a) assimilation
   b) acculturation
   c) psychological process
   d) social process

4. Foreign students who are characterized by confusion and disintegration as the individual confronts new values, behavior, beliefs, and lifestyles are experiencing:
   a) culture shock
   b) social process
   c) crisis stage
   d) honeymoon stage

5. A foreign student's accuracy of understanding of what is going on in one's social environment is referred to as:
   a) application of behavior
   b) level of mere adequacy
   c) clarity of mental frame of reference
   d) a and b

6. The feeling of ambiguity and loss of personal status when one tries to transfer one's present role into a new cultural environment and function within that role is referred to as:
   a) cultural fatigue
   b) culture shock
   c) role shock
   d) educational shock

7. Therapy aimed at foreign students to change negative, self-defeating thoughts to help the individual recognize the association between dysfunctional thinking and his or her own feeling and behavior is called:
   a) directive
   b) cognitive
   c) psychoanalytical
   d) none of the above

8. A process involving the state of loss and disorientation requiring adjustment similar to that experienced during any change in one's familiar environment is referred to as:
   a) acculturation
   b) intercultural adjustment
   c) cultural accommodation
   d) transition shock

9. To enhance counselor credibility in counseling foreign students and to be consistent with the expectation of the clients, the counselor must:
   a) speak the same language
   b) study foreign behavior
   c) modify counseling styles
   d) a and b

10. Values that emphasize centrality and autonomy are referred to by Thomas (1985) as:
    a) Western psychology
    b) Eastern psychology
    c) ecological strategy
    d) individualistic strategy

Case Studies

1. A Middle Eastern student attending a university on the East Coast was experiencing a difficult time meeting American students. One day after his chemistry class, he decided to talk with a student who sat next to him in class. The classmate was an American female who easily engaged in a conversation with the Middle Eastern student. After a few minutes of conversing, the American student on several occasions glanced at her watch. The Middle Eastern student noticed her behavior and felt as though he was intruding or boring her with his conversation.

   On another occasion, the Middle Eastern student was having lunch at the campus cafeteria. While he was eating, he noticed that many American students were eating and reading at the same time. Others were eating and writing letters or doing their school work. He found it very interesting that American students rarely relaxed.

2. Pélin, an international student from Taiwan, was asked to share her experience with students who had recently arrived in the United States from China. Pélin shared that when she first arrived she was excited about attending an American university. In her spare time she went to see American movies and ate a variety of American foods. After some time she began noticing the major differences between the behavior of American students and her own and how their beliefs, values, and lifestyles conflicted with hers.

   Pélin lived in a residence hall and had an American roommate. She spoke of how offended and embarrassed she was when her roommate's boyfriend came by to visit and they openly kissed and hugged each other. She also shared the difficulty she experienced when using the community showers for women. Her sense of privacy and personal space was constantly being challenged.

   Pélin shared with the group that, at first, her adjustment as a student at an American university was difficult, but although many of the values were different from hers, she was able to adjust. Pélin ended with saying that her biggest growth was being able to appreciate her own values by learning to appreciate American values.

Classroom Activities

ORIENTATION FOR A CROSS-CULTURAL EXPERIENCE
Adapted from "Dress Rehearsal for a Cross-Cultural Experience," by Robert T. Moran, Josef A. Mestenhauser, and Paul B. Pedersen, *International Educational and Cultural Exchange*, Summer, 1974, by permission

Objective

To define the kinds of roles that are important for persons new to a culture, and to learn whether their suggested solutions to problems are appropriate to their new culture.

Procedure

1. Participants should be provided with the following list of images that persons from other cultures could manifest (others may be added). Each image should be discussed and clarified by a facilitator or instructor.

- Internationalist/nationalist
- Traditionalist/progressive
- Insider/visitor guest
- Deserving/poor
- Disoriented/oriented
- Competitor
- Culture sharer
- Elite

2. Participants are to select three images from the list that they feel are most appropriate to themselves most of the time.

3. Participants are then provided with problems and five solutions, prepared ahead of time by the facilitator. Participants are to select from the five solutions the one that most appeals to them and is consistent with the three images they have already selected. Following are two examples of problems and solutions within the image contexts.

Example 1: "Insider/visitor guest"

A foreign student had an argument with his host family. He felt that the whole family was demanding too much of his time and attention. The family in turn felt the guest was being discourteous and demanding special treatment that they would not give to their own children. The arguments became so oppressive that they affected the student's grades.

Alternatives
1. I would make some excuse and leave the host family and find another place to live.

2. I would confront the host family and tell them that they were taking too much of my time and that I need more time to study.

3. I would rearrange my schedule and try to study more at the university and continue to let the family take up time.

4. I would do nothing, accept it, and do my best in school.

5. Or I would _____

Example 2: "Disoriented/oriented"
A foreign person fails in his attempt to mix socially with Americans and puts the blame on his ethnic identity. He debases the values of his own culture and rejects his countrymen, who in turn reject him. At the same time he is not more successful in communicating with Americans. He is isolated and feels lonely.

Alternatives
1. I would accept living in a foreign country and realize I will be lonely.

2. I would seek help, preferably from other countrymen and counselors.

3. I would socialize with people from my own country and try to show them the stupidity of our values.

4. I would start over and try to mix socially with another group of Americans.

5. Or I would _____

4. Participants then discuss each other's solutions in terms of whether or not they feel the solution helps or hinders the person's image and is appropriate to the situation.

5. Roles appropriate to the problems are assigned and the problems are role-played.

6. After the role-playing, each person is allowed to defend his or her position and a vote is taken of all participants regarding the best overall solution.

7. Participants may then form small groups (eight to 10 persons) and develop their own set of problems to solve with accompanying discussion, role-playing, and voting to rehearse solutions to their own present and future problems.

Insight
Each multicultural situation presents choices: some better and some worse.

MICHIGAN INTERNATIONAL STUDENT PROBLEM INVENTORY

Adapted from the "Michigan International Student Problem Inventory," by John W. Porter and A. O. Haller (printed by International Programs, Michigan State University, East Lansing, Michigan, 1962), by permission

Objective

To define problems or areas of conflict that an international student may experience.

Procedure

The following directions should be read to a group of international students: You are not being tested. There are no right or wrong answers. This is a list of statements about situations that occasionally trouble (perturb, distress, annoy, grieve, or worry) students from other countries who are attending college in the United States. The statements are related to admissions, academic work, language, religion, and so forth. Please follow these steps:

Step 1. Read the list of statements carefully, pause at each statement, and if it suggests a situation that is troubling you, circle the number to the left of the statement.

Step 2. After completing Step 1, go back over the numbers you have circled and place an X in the circle of the statements that are of most concern to you.

---

1. Evaluation of my former school credentials
2. Concern about value of U.S. education
3. Choosing college subjects
4. Treatment received at orientation meetings
5. Unfavorable remarks about home country
6. Concept of being a "foreign" student
7. Frequent college examinations
8. Compulsory class attendance
9. Writing or typing term (semester) papers
10. Concern about becoming too "Westernized"
11. Insufficient personal-social counseling
12. Being in love with someone
13. Taste of food in the United States
14. Problems regarding housing
15. Being told where one must live
16. Poor eyesight
17. Recurrent headaches
18. Physical height and physique
19. Religious practice in the United States
20. Attending church socials
21. Concern about my religious beliefs
22. Speaking English
23. Giving oral reports in class
24. Ability to write English
25. Regulations on student activities
26. Treatment received at social functions
27. Relationship of men and women in the United States
28. Lack of money to meet expenses
29. Not receiving enough money from home
30. Having to do manual labor (with hands)

31.	Finding a job upon returning home	32.	Not enough time in the United States to study
33.	Trying to extend stay in the United States	34.	Getting admitted to a U.S. college
35.	Registration for classes each term	36.	Not attending college of my first choice
37.	Relationship with foreign student advisor	38.	Leisure-time activities of U.S. students
39.	Law-enforcement practices in the United States	40.	Competitive college grading system
41.	Objective examinations (true-false, etc.)	42.	Insufficient advice from academic advisor
43.	Being lonely	44.	Feeling inferior to others
45.	Trying to make friends	46.	Costs of buying food
47.	Insufficient clothing	48.	Not being able to room with U.S. student
49.	Hard to hear	50.	Nervousness
51.	Finding adequate health services	52.	Finding worship group of own faith
53.	Christianity as a philosophy	54.	Variety of religious faiths in the United States
55.	Reciting in class	56.	Understanding lectures in English
57.	Reading textbooks in English	58.	Dating practices of U.S. people
59.	Being accepted in social groups	60.	Not being able to find "dates"
61.	Saving enough money for social events	62.	Immigration work restrictions
63.	Limited amount U.S. dollar will purchase	64.	Becoming a citizen of the United States
65.	Changes in home government	66.	Desire to not return to home country
67.	Understanding college catalogs	68.	Immigration regulations
69.	Lack of knowledge about the United States	70.	Campus size
71.	U.S. emphasis on time and promptness	72.	Understanding how to use the library
73.	Too many interferences with studies	74.	Feel unprepared for U.S. college work
75.	Concerned about grades	76.	Sexual customs in the United States
77.	Homesickness	78.	Feeling superior to others
79.	Bathroom facilities cause problems	80.	Distance to classes from residence
81.	Relationship with roommate	82.	Dietary problems
83.	Need more time to rest	84.	Worried about mental health

85.	Having time to devote to own religion	86.	Spiritual versus materialistic values
87.	Doubting the value of any religion	88.	Understanding U.S. slang
89.	Limited English vocabulary	90.	Pronunciation not understood
91.	Activities of international houses	92.	U.S. emphasis on sports
93.	Problems when shopping in U.S.	94.	Finding part-time work
95.	Unexpected financial needs	96.	Money for clothing
97.	Uncertainties in the world today	98.	Desire to enroll at another college
99.	U.S. education not what was expected	100.	Differences in purposes among U.S. colleges
101.	Difference in education in the United States and at home	102.	Not being met on arrival at campus
103.	College orientation program sufficient	104.	Trying to be a student and a tourist
105.	Attitude of some foreign students	106.	Doing laboratory assignments
107.	Insufficient personal help from professors	108.	Relationship between U.S. students and faculty
109.	U.S. emphasis on personal habits of cleanliness	110.	Not feeling at ease in public
111.	Attitude of some U.S. people to skin color	112.	Finding a place to live between college terms
113.	Changes in weather conditions	114.	Lack of invitations
115.	Feeling tension	116.	Service received at health center
117.	Health suffering because of academic pace	118.	Criticisms of homeland's religion
119.	Accepting differences in great religions	120.	Confusion about religion and morals in the United States
121.	Insufficient remedial English services	122.	Having a non-English speaking roommate
123.	Holding a conversation with U.S. friend	124.	Activities of foreign student organization
125.	Lack of opportunities to meet more U.S. "ambassador" people	126.	Concern about political discussions
127.	Costs of an automobile	128.	Finding employment between college terms
129.	Finding jobs that pay well	130.	Insufficient help from placement office
131.	Staying in the United States and getting a job	132.	Wonder if U.S. education is useful for job at home

Insight

Some problems occur to international students with greater frequency than others.

CHAPTER 10

COUNSELING REFUGEES: THE NORTH AMERICAN EXPERIENCE

The tenth chapter, by Harriet P. Lefley, reviews the extensive literature on counseling refugees from a variety of different backgrounds. The considerable differences among refugees have sometimes disguised the patterns of similarities across cultures for persons with refugee status. The effects of violence and conflict, for example, are almost universally present as a unifying issue.

Discussion Questions

1. Discuss the four domains in which expertise is required for counseling refugees.

2. What are the required "tasks and skills over and above those applied to other groups" that Lefley contends are required for counseling refugees?

3. Discuss Berry's (1986) four distinct varieties of acculturation as they relate to refugees.

4. Why might refugees be reluctant to seek out help from a counselor?

5. What family problems are more likely to occur among refugees and how might counseling apply to those problems?

6. Discuss some of the interventions suggested by Lefley for working with refugees.

7. What might be some advantages of systems therapy as compared to individual counseling therapy in working with refugees?

8. What is the danger of developing counseling models for working with refugees based on maladjustment, dysfunction, or psychopathology?

9. How might a counselor emphasize positive adaptive skills that focus on the strengths of a refugee client?

10. Discuss the importance of coordinating and integrating different community services for counseling refugees.

Multiple Choice Questions

1. A subset of immigrants who have come under duress, to escape situations perceived as politically, economically, psychologically, and physically threatening to survival is referred to as:
   a) undocumented aliens
   b) exiles
   c) entrants
   d) all of the above

2. A model in which the focus is acquiring the salient characteristics of a culture rather than the psychological adjustment to a new culture is called:
   a) acculturation model
   b) mainstreaming model
   c) assimilation model
   d) culture-learning model

3. According to Berry (1986) the withdrawal from the mainstream and maintenance of a segregated cultural identity is called:
   a) deculturation
   b) culture shock
   c) rejection
   d) assimilation

4. Antonovsky (1979) noted that the crucial variable in successful adaptation was not the content of culture and social structure but its:
   a) value system
   b) time orientation
   c) religion
   d) relative stability

5. Westermeyer's (1986) research on refugee populations found that the highest rates of psychiatric disorders occur in what year following migration:
   a) half year
   b) first year
   c) fifth year
   d) tenth year

6. An Indochinese refugee who describes feelings of constant chill, dresses more warmly than necessary, and self-diagnoses the chill as flu or malaria is experiencing:
   a) hyperthermia
   b) frigophobia
   c) somatic disorders
   d) all of the above

7. A major source of conflict among refugees is:
   a) erosion of family structure
   b) modernization
   c) social isolation
   d) acculturation

8. Approaches to counseling refugees should eschew notions of:
   a) psychopathology
   b) coping
   c) stress
   d) adaptation

9. A popular home remedy used by refugees to cure frigophobia is called:
   a) rubbing out the wind
   b) *espiritismo*
   c) *santeria*
   d) b and c

10. In helping refugee clients cope with ambiguities and frustrations counselors should utilize cultural variables that foster:
   a) behavior skills
   b) cognitive skills
   c) adaptive skills
   d) a, b, and c

Case Studies

1. An admissions counselor at a California state university was reviewing an admissions application submitted by a Vietnamese refugee student. Sections of the admissions application requested parental information and contained specific questions about the family history. Because these sections were left blank, the student was requested to make an appointment with the admissions counselor.

During their meeting the counselor learned that the student and his sister were living with an aunt, and they had no knowledge of the existence of their parents. The student hesitantly shared with the counselor that his parents had been taken as prisoners by the Communist regime in Vietnam, and he had been left behind with his younger sister. Through VIA and the refugee program, the student was able to locate his aunt in California.

It had been 10 years since he had last seen his parents. The student expressed that it was important for him to go to college because with a college degree he would be able to take care of his younger sister and not be such a burden to his aunt.

2. A Hispanic social worker in Colorado was assigned a client who had been raped by her employer. The client was a 25-year-old Mexican woman who had come to the United States so that she could work and save money to pay for an operation that her son needed.

The client had answered an ad in the paper to work as a live-in nanny. The employer was a successful dentist, married, with two children. Within days after the Mexican woman had started working, she was raped by the dentist. Unable to speak English and fearful of the consequences of deportation, the woman did not report the incident to authorities. In desperation, the woman went to a priest for help. The priest contacted a clinic, which later contacted the social work agency. It was discovered that the woman had been raped on 11 different occasions within a five-day period.

Classroom Activities

CULTURAL BIAS
Adapted from "Cross-Cultural Concepts," an unpublished manuscript by Anne Pedersen

Objective
To become aware of different ways to approach a situation. One important barrier to cross-cultural communication is one's own cultural bias. If we are limited to understanding all other people from our own cultural point of view, then we are trapped by a limited and rigid set of rules.

Procedure

Copies of the following list are handed out to members of the group. Each participant is to circle five adjectives describing people they like, and underline five adjectives describing people they do not like to be around. Participants may add adjectives of their own. Wherever possible, the adjectives should be related to specific cultural groups.

adventurous	good listener	shy
affectionate	helpful	soft on subordinates
ambitious	independent	stern
appreciative	indifferent to others	submissive
argumentative	intolerant	successful
competitive	jealous	sympathetic
complaining	kind	tactful
considerate of others	loud	talkative
discourteous	neat	teasing
distant	needs much praise	thorough
dominating	obedient	thoughtful
easily angered	optimistic	touchy, cannot be kidded
easily discouraged	orderly	trusting
easily influenced	rebellious	uncommunicative
efficient	responsible	understanding
enthusiastic	sarcastic	varied interests
false	self-centered	very dependent on others
forgiving	self-respecting	warm
fun-loving	self-satisfied	well-mannered
gives praise readily	shrewd, devious	willing worker

Insight

We each have our own cultural biases.

CULTURE SHOCK LADDER RATINGS AND SYMPTOM CHECKLIST
Thomas Coffman, 1978, by permission

Objective

To help students measure the presence or absence of symptoms of culture shock in their own lives.

Procedure

1. The ladder below represents a set of positions ranging from life at its worst (0) to life at its best (10), as viewed by the student personally. Participants are to indicate where on the ladder they feel they stand personally at the present time, all things considered.

```
10----------------------10
 9---------------------- 9
 8---------------------- 8
 7---------------------- 7
 6---------------------- 6
 5---------------------- 5
 4---------------------- 4
 3---------------------- 3
 2---------------------- 2
 1---------------------- 1
 0---------------------- 0
```

2. How often in the past two weeks or so have you experienced the following reactions or feelings? (Students should circle their responses, from 0 to 4, for each item.)

	Not at All	Rarely	Occasionally	Frequently	Almost Always
Anxious (worried or fearful about something)	0	1	2	3	4
Depressed (unhappy, moody)	0	1	2	3	4
Sleep problems	0	1	2	3	4
Digestion, elimination problems	0	1	2	3	4
Tired, fatigued	0	1	2	3	4
Angry, irritable, impatient	0	1	2	3	4
Lonely	0	1	2	3	4
Forgetfulness	0	1	2	3	4
Hard time concentrating	0	1	2	3	4
Feeling of being "different," not fitting in or belonging	0	1	2	3	4
Nostalgia for remembered pleasures	0	1	2	3	4

Insight

A person may be experiencing more -- or less -- culture shock than he or she imagines.

CHAPTER 11

BEHAVIORAL APPROACHES TO COUNSELING ACROSS CULTURES

The eleventh chapter, by Junko Tanaka-Matsumi and H. Nick Higginbotham, integrates the extensive literature about behavioral counseling and its use across cultures. The chapter describes how a counselor can identify appropriate reinforcing events and interpret culturally different behaviors accurately across cultures.

Discussion Questions

1. Discuss how culture can be considered part of one's social environment.

2. Compare and contrast the medical model and applied behavior analysis for counseling across cultures.

3. What special problems are likely to arise in applying the functional analysis of behavior to a client from another culture?

4. Why is the training of personnel to demonstrate competency in cultural assessment one of the most important goals of behavior modification?

5. Discuss the ability of behavior therapy to empirically evaluate environment and person conditions and monitor the degree of behavior change produced by treatment in cross-cultural counseling.

6. How do the authors of this chapter explain the failures in cross-cultural counseling from a behavioral perspective?

7. To what extent is behavior therapy "embedded in the ideology of modernity and the values of modern technological society"?

8. How do the authors explain the failure of counseling to work with minority groups and how might behaviorism overcome those failures?

9. What are some unique advantages of behavioral counseling for work with foreign students and overseas sojourners?

10. What are some unique advantages of behavioral counseling for work with refugees?

Multiple Choice Questions

1. A theoretical focus that concentrates on the direct change of overt behavior rather than the underlying or disease factors that produce symptomatic behaviors is referred to as:
   a) multimodal therapy
   b) systems therapy
   c) behavior modification
   d) Gestalt therapy

2. Applied behavior analysis analyses the relationship between:
   a) man and universe
   b) religion and values
   c) behavior and culture
   d) person and environment

3. The focus on maladaptive behaviors as symptoms of an underlying illness is referred to as the:
   a) psychoanalytical model
   b) medical model
   c) Jungian model
   d) Rogerian model

4. In functional analysis of behavior, pinpointing the person's specific presenting problem is called:
   a) diagnostic assessment
   b) identifying controlling stimuli
   c) problem solving
   d) selection of target behavior

5. Szasz (1961) argued that mental illness is a:
   a) disease
   b) myth
   c) cultural element
   d) a and b

6. According to Wolf (1978) the notion that incorporates social criteria for evaluating the treatment focus, procedures, and effects is called:
   a) identifying controlling stimuli
   b) social intervention
   c) social validation
   d) none of the above

7. A method that enhances the therapist's social influence in the identification of variables that evoke client expectations of positive treatment is called:
   a) client variables
   b) situation-outcome expectancy
   c) counselor variables
   d) social variables

8. In behavior therapy no behavior in itself is considered:
   a) normal/abnormal
   b) a disease
   c) universal
   d) all of the above

9. According to Mikulas (1981) what religion parallels behavior modification in that both emphasize an objective and practical approach to current problem solving:
   a) Hinduism
   b) Catholicism
   c) Protestantism
   d) Buddhism

10. Overseas sojourners and foreign students experience culture shock. A remedy for culture shock involves:
a) social learning
b) English as a second language
c) Psychotherapy
d) All of the above

Case Studies

1. A counselor at a rehabilitation center for juveniles was assigned to a case in which a minor had a history of aggressive behavior. The minor was sent to the rehabilitation center for eight months because of prior history and violation of probation. After a few counseling sessions the counselor and the minor were able to identify situations that caused the minor to act in an aggressive manner. It was learned in the counseling sessions that the minor as a young child witnessed his father physically abuse his mother. The minor described his father as a man who had a short fuse and vented his anger at his mother.

The minor internalized his feelings and developed an intense hatred toward his father. The minor grew up not knowing how to deal with his anger and would act out when confronted with stressful situations. Through additional counseling it was discovered that the minor had an uncle that he respected very highly and always called whenever he was in trouble. The minor shared with the counselor that his uncle was someone who was always there when the minor needed someone to talk to. The uncle was the the mother's older brother; he was self-employed and often traveled.

Through further counseling the minor and the counselor were able to develop strategies to deal with the minor's behavior when confronted with stressful situations. Rewards were granted in the form of additional visitation time with his mother on Sundays when the minor was able to control his anger. The minor received training in breathing exercises to help him control his emotions in a stressful event. The counselor also arranged special visits with the minor's uncle. In addition the counselor worked with the minor's mother in learning pro-social skills in preparation for the minor's release.

2. A married couple met with a counselor to discuss the difficulties they were having with their oldest daughter. The daughter was 15 years old and a sophomore in high school. The parents' primary concern was that the daughter was always yelling at her parents and was in total control of her life. The parents had no control of their own daughter.

The counselor spoke to the parents in detail about areas that could be worked on, but the parents would be required to participate in learning anger-control skills. The parents were hesitant and shared with the counselor that it would be difficult to take part actively in the process.

The counselor explained to the parents that attempting to change behavior required the commitment of all parties that interact within the client's environment. The parents did not think it was possible because both parents worked and were involved in several community activities and had little time to spare.

Classroom Activities

DIALOGUE WITHIN OURSELVES

Objective
To gain practice in listening to and making cultural interpretations of "internal dialogue" of others on specific cross-cultural issues that generate ambivalent thoughts and feelings.

Procedure
1. Participants are to select a cross-cultural subject that produces ambivalent thoughts and feelings within themselves.

2. Participants next tune in on their ambivalent thoughts and listen to the two sides of their internal dialogue.

3. Participants write down the dialogue between their internal voices as a script of a play or conversation, attempting to identify the emergence of cultural bias.

Insight
Our internal dialogue is often a discussion between positive and negative voices.

A SIMULATION DESIGNING EXERCISE: "MULTIPOLY"

Objective
To simulate intercultural interaction with a small group working together to design and play an intercultural situation or event on a game board. The process involved with this activity is quite serious and will demand considerable investment of time and energy but will, it is hoped, result in a product both stimulating and useful in a group or organization.

Procedure
The rules for a well-known board game should be rewritten to fit the conditions of six different ethnic, racial, or cultural roles. The "rules" for each role will differ in this game, as they do in real life. Participants should be sensitive to the different advantages and disadvantages facing each role, to the different aspirations and goals to which each role aspires, to the different acceptable and unacceptable ways of doing things for each role, and to the different "style" that applies not only to each role group as perceived by themselves but also as perceived by outsiders. Each participant should ask himself or herself, for example:

o Does each of the six groups have the same ultimate goal? Money? Influence? Popularity? Power?

o Does each group begin the game with the same resources in terms of money, power, or opportunity?

When the project is complete there will be *six different sets of rules* for the game and all will be able to play the same game together *simultaneously*, each of the six players being guided by a different set of rules.

The name of the game should be changed to Multipoly or some other more appropriate (and not registered) title, as for example, "Multiculturalism." Different sets of rules should be drawn up independently. Then the participants should divide into groups of six persons, one for each role, to coordinate their ideas into one set of rules for that role.

The place names on the game board should also be indigenized, and new sets of "Chance" and "Community Chest" cards developed to fit the situation being simulated. The steps for designing the game are as follows:

1. Identify policy objectives for each culture being represented.

2. Identify intercultural situations where the participating cultures are likely to interact for each space around the edge of the game board.

3. Identify the problems each situation would create for each participating culture and assign a negative score to the space.

4. Identify the opportunities each situation would create for each participating culture and assign a positive score to the space.

5. Assign a net positive or a net negative score and consequence for each participating culture relative to each situation.

6. Identify additional solutions through the "Chance" or "Community Chest" type decks of cards available to players landing on designated spaces.

7. Design each participating culture role to accurately reflect the balance of feasibility and cost-benefit testing of alternative choices interacting with the other cultures in society.

8. Design the game so that a player in one culture role will finish the game knowing more of that culture's role in society than previously.

9. Design the game so that a player in one culture role will see the advantages and disadvantages of meeting the needs of other cultures outside the person's own group through cooperation.

10. Provide opportunities for discussion of how the system could be changed toward a more equitable distribution of opportunities across racial and cultural MULTIPOLY.

(The situations should be filled in for this game board)

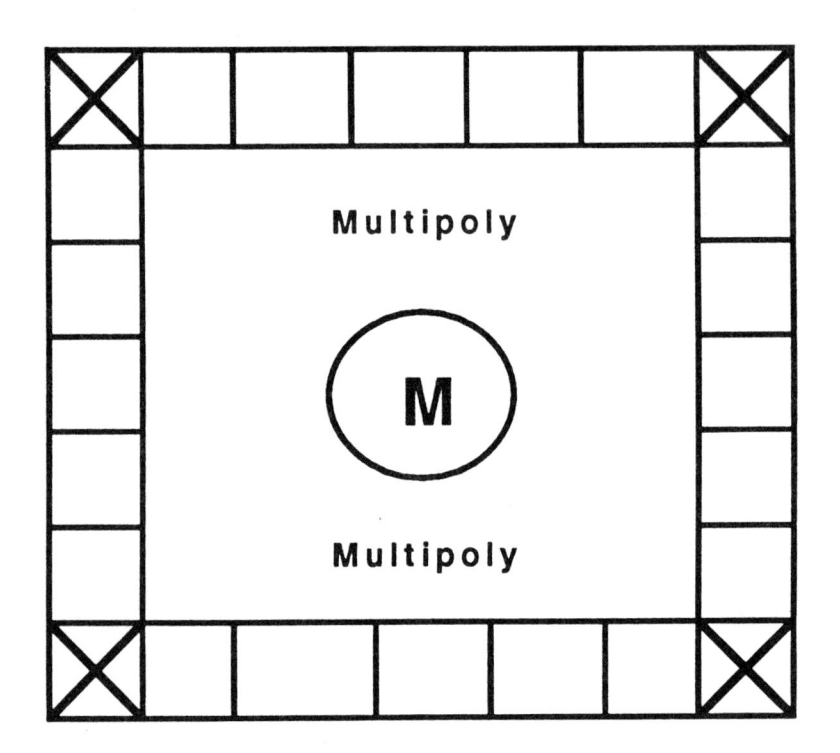

Insight
    Each culturally defined role has different advantages and disadvantages for each situation.

CHAPTER 12

ASSESSMENT IN CROSS-CULTURAL COUNSELING

The twelfth chapter, by Walter J. Lonner and Farah A. Ibrahim, reviews the problems and opportunities associated with the use of psychological tests and related data-gathering devices that may be useful in counseling across cultures. The many implicit and explicit biases in tests and measures require skilled interpretation by counselors in culturally different settings.

Discussion Questions

1. Discuss the authors' recommendation that each individual client be viewed as a unique "cultural reality."

2. How will the SAWV help you assess a client's worldview and how would that contribute to the counseling process?

3. What are the problems of ethnocentricity implicit in "armchair" diagnosis in cross-cultural counseling?

4. Discuss the implications of the statement that cultural bias is inherent in the cross-cultural use of all tests.

5. Discuss Berry's (1972) notion of "radical cultural relativism" as it applies to the use of tests and measures across cultures.

6. Discuss the four types of equivalence typically used to describe measures that are developed in one culture and applied to a different culture.

7. Discuss the different ways and methods that have been used to reduce a Euroamerican bias in psychological assessment instruments.

8. Select one of the specific measurement instruments described in this chapter and discuss its usefulness in cross-cultural counseling.

9. How might a counselor use nonstandardized assessment in counseling across cultures?

10. Suppose you are assigned the task of assessing a non-English-speaking foreign student who *seems* to be somewhat disturbed. What are some of the more important things you should take into consideration before, during, and after the assessment process?

Multiple Choice Questions

1. Marsella, Kinzie, and Gordon (1973) noted that the expression of mental disorders in different cultures varies according to the concept of:
   a) community
   b) self
   c) religion
   d) acculturation

2. Psychological tests that depend upon empirically established relationships and are not necessarily associated with any particular psychological theory are referred to as:
   a) construct referenced
   b) criterion referenced
   c) qualitative research
   d) quantitative research

3. Berry (1972) referred to the conservative solution of developing tests based on locally conceived (within-culture) constructs, with locally valid criteria to "prove" the existence of the construct as:
   a) *obugezi*
   b) cross-cultural
   c) radical cultural relativism
   d) none of the above

4. In establishing equivalence in testing, the concern with the meaning that persons attach to specific stimuli such as test items is called:
   a) metric equivalence
   b) functional equivalence
   c) back-translation
   d) conceptional equivalence

5. In testing, a factor that predisposes a client to respond in ways that appear unique to a United States psychologist or counselor is referred to as:
   a) social desirability
   b) cultural assimilation
   c) desired state
   d) response set

6. A scale that assesses a client's belief whether achievement and autonomy or (lack of it) is due to internal or external fact is referred to as the:
   a) system of multicultural pluralistic assessment
   b) Cattell Culture-Fair Intelligence Test
   c) State-Trait Anxiety Inventory
   d) Locus of Control Scale

7. There are two specific approaches to the assessment of a client's worldview. One assessment tool is the Scale to Access World View (SAWV); the other is:
   a) Minnesota Multiphasic Personality Inventory
   b) Goal Attainment Scaling
   c) Locus of Control Scale
   d) none of the above

8. A method of nonstandardized approaches that include daily and weekly logs, autobiography, and biographical inventory is called:
   a) anxiety disorder interview schedule
   b) self-observation measures
   c) self-report awareness
   d) diagnostic interview schedule

9. The most widely used device to measure "anxiety" across cultures is called:
   a) *Diagnostic and Statistical Manual*
   b) Beck Depression Inventory
   c) Depression Adjective Checklist
   d) State-Trait Anxiety Inventory

10. In "generic" counseling and psychotherapy the closet theorist of what the client experiences as a shared worldview is:
    a) Freud
    b) Perls
    c) Rogers
    d) Ellis

Case Studies

1. In a small community in Texas, parents of Mexican-American children were upset when several of the students were placed in a specialized classroom designed for children with learning disabilities. Several parents received a letter from the teacher stating that their child had been given a standardized intelligence test and the results were very low.

   The letter stated that the exam provided evidence that their child was borderline mentally retarded. After much pressure from the parents, consultants from a university evaluated the exam and found that the intelligence test was biased. The test itself did not take into account both linguistic and cultural factors of the students that were tested.

   The students were retested with an intelligence test that was not biased and was sensitive to linguistic and cultural elements. The results of the exam indicated that intelligence levels of the Mexican-American students did not differ from those of white-Anglo students; in several areas the Mexican-American students scored higher than their counterparts.

2. An Afro-American woman met with a counselor because she was feeling depressed about being unemployed. The client expressed that she felt worthless and useless. Unemployed for the past four months, she could not understand why, with a business degree and four years of professional experience, she had been unable to find a job.

   The client stated that for the past three months she had been sending out six resumés a week and had not received any responses. The woman had begun to question her own ability and self-confidence and had begun to feel that she did not have the "right stuff."

The counselor responded to the client by saying that the factors for her being unemployed were beyond her control. The counselor went on to say that she was not the only person who was unemployed and that companies throughout the nation were laying off people because of the depressed state of the economy. The woman sat in silence. The counselor knew that she was experiencing difficulty accepting what he had told her.

Classroom Activities

THE CRITICAL INCIDENT TECHNIQUE

Objective

To bring an actual experience or event into the classroom or training program as a resource. The incident is "critical," meaning important, essential, or valuable, in the way that a part of a machine might be critical to the smooth operation of the machine. The incident is a short description of an event that did or could take place within a five- or 10-minute time period, approximately. A case study, by contrast, is much more complicated and might take place over weeks, months, or even years. Critical incidents are based on real-life situations and typically involve a "dilemma" where there is no easy or obvious solution. The objective of critical incidents is to stimulate thinking about basic and important issues that occur in real life situations. By reviewing the incident, participants can imagine themselves in the same situation, develop strategies to deal with that situation, and become more realistic in their expectations. Rehearsing what a participant would do in a critical incident in the relative safety of a training situation requires limited risk-taking and yet provides much of the complexity of real-life situations. Critical incidents do not necessarily imply a single solution or "right way" of resolving the dilemma in the situation, but explore alternative solutions and their implications.

Procedure

Critical incidents are generated in small groups. Participants typically organize into five-person groups to discuss the issues involved, identifying the advantages and disadvantages of each solution and additional information that might be needed before a single best solution is selected. Each critical incident may require from a half hour to an hour to discuss. Each group should have a reporter to take notes on the discussion. After the discussion each group should report back to the larger plenary group the results of their discussion. After all groups have reported back to the larger group, an open discussion of all critical incidents will help participants to identify their own implicit biases and assumptions. The critical incident format typically includes five elements, which the group should perform to generate the incident.

1. Identify the event or occurrence with as much specificity as possible: the problem to be solved, the issue involved, etc.

2. Describe the relevant details and circumstances surrounding the event, so that participants will understand what happened. (What? When? How? Why? Where?)

3. List the people involved. Describe them and their relationships to you and to one another.

4. Describe your own role in the situation (what you did, how you acted) and identify the particular cross-cultural skill or skills involved. What would you do differently the next time? Describe your interpretation of events.

5. Write a brief analysis of the incident. Tell what you learned from the experience and state your estimate of the level of development of your particular cross-cultural skills as you reflect on the incident.

The following questions can be used to begin discussion:

1. What are the issues that need to be considered before the individual can make a decision in this situation?

2. What are the possible solutions to this situation?

Critical incidents are particularly popular in training about multicultural relationships. In part this is because there are few, if any, other measures that can be used accurately or appropriately across different cultural groups. In part, it is because critical incidents include the complexity of real-life situations where persons from more than one culture come into contact. The critical incident can be used to develop the following multicultural skills:

1. Information source development: the ability to use many information sources within a social or cultural environment. The student should work to develop information-gathering skills such as observing, questioning the people one meets, and listening carefully.

2. Cultural understanding: the ability to be aware of and understand the values, feelings, and attitudes of people in another culture and the ways in which these influence behavior, or, reversing it, to observe behaviors and define the values and attitudes that undergird the behaviors.

3. Interpersonal communication: the ability to listen well, speak clearly, and also pay attention to the expression of nonverbal communication, such as the messages delivered through physical movements, eyes, facial expressions, and the whole range of meanings developed through face-to-face encounter.

4. Commitment to persons and relationships: the ability to become involved deeply with people beyond superficial relationships, giving and inspiring trust and confidence, establishing a basis for mutual liking and respect, caring enough for them and acting in ways that are both truthful for the student and sensitive toward the feelings of others.

5. Decision Making: the ability to come to conclusions, based on assessment of the information available, and to take action. This might also be called problem solving, which includes learning to be explicit about the problem, working out steps to a solution, and generating alternatives. In the cross-cultural situation, it is important to be able to identify what is at issue, the dimensions of the problem, and alternatives that are personally acceptable and culturally acceptable as well.

Insight

Learning from experience can be a valuable and safe part of classroom learning.

THE I.I.P. QUESTIONNAIRE
Developed by Paul B. Pedersen, John Lewis, and James Campbell, Syracuse University. All rights reserved by James Campbell, John Lewis, and Paul B. Pedersen, Syracuse University, January 1984

Objective

To measure how the same situation may be seen differently before and after training in multicultural counseling.

Procedure

Students should fill in the following information before completing the questionnaire. A pseudonym or symbol may be used instead of the student's name. The same pseudonym or symbol should be used on the post-test.

Name_____Institution_____
Date_____

Number of years as a practicing counselor or psychologist (please circle):
    under 1 yr   1-3 yrs   4-6 yrs   7-10 yrs   over 10 yrs

Number of courses taken in counseling or related field (please circle):
    1 course   2-5 courses   6-10 courses   over 10 courses

Main area of professional interest_____

    Please specify (circle one):

    pre-test   post-test

For each incident or situation, students should indicate the degree to which they feel the problem is interpersonal, intercultural, or psychopathological in nature, using the definitions of these terms as they currently understand them.

    1 = a totally irrelevant issue in respect to this problem
    10 = an extremely important issue in respect to this problem

1. A 35-year-old man lives in a crowded neighborhood in a downtown city area, yet feels isolated and alone. He feels people are cold and unfriendly.

    Interpersonal: 1 2 3 4 5 6 7 8 9 10
    Intercultural: 1 2 3 4 5 6 7 8 9 10
    Psychopathological: 1 2 3 4 5 6 7 8 9 10

2. A female college student feels that men are only interested in sex and not in getting to know her as an individual. Although she admits to being very flirtatious, she feels angry and degraded when men respond in a sexual way.

    Interpersonal: 1 2 3 4 5 6 7 8 9 10
    Intercultural: 1 2 3 4 5 6 7 8 9 10
    Psychopathological: 1 2 3 4 5 6 7 8 9 10

3. A case worker indicates to a client (male, head of household) that the client will need to do some of the work that is needed to find him an apartment and a job. The client is angry and resentful because he feels the caseworker should be doing all these things for him.

    Interpersonal: 1 2 3 4 5 6 7 8 9 10
    Intercultural: 1 2 3 4 5 6 7 8 9 10
    Psychopathological: 1 2 3 4 5 6 7 8 9 10

4. A 28-year-old, unmarried woman is extremely reluctant to make any decision without the permission of her father and his full support.

    Interpersonal: 1 2 3 4 5 6 7 8 9 10
    Intercultural: 1 2 3 4 5 6 7 8 9 10
    Psychopathological: 1 2 3 4 5 6 7 8 9 10

5. A 23-year-old woman engages in premarital sex for the first time. She subsequently comes to a counselor, suffering from guilt and the fear that she will be viewed by her friends and family as promiscuous.

    Interpersonal: 1 2 3 4 5 6 7 8 9 10
    Intercultural: 1 2 3 4 5 6 7 8 9 10
    Psychopathological: 1 2 3 4 5 6 7 8 9 10

6. A Korean woman has a baby in a New York hospital; all aspects of the delivery are normal. The woman soon becomes depressed as well as feeling angry and resentful toward the hospital staff.

    Interpersonal: 1 2 3 4 5 6 7 8 9 10
    Intercultural: 1 2 3 4 5 6 7 8 9 10
    Psychopathological: 1 2 3 4 5 6 7 8 9 10

7. A person is referred for counseling because he keeps losing jobs due to absenteeism and tardiness.

   Interpersonal: 1 2 3 4 5 6 7 8 9 10
   Intercultural: 1 2 3 4 5 6 7 8 9 10
   Psychopathological: 1 2 3 4 5 6 7 8 9 10

8. A person goes to a counselor for help in choosing a career. As the counselor tries to help the client clarify his feelings and attitudes about different careers, the client becomes angry and frustrated.

   Interpersonal: 1 2 3 4 5 6 7 8 9 10
   Intercultural: 1 2 3 4 5 6 7 8 9 10
   Psychopathological: 1 2 3 4 5 6 7 8 9 10

9. A person is referred for counseling because he reports having secret conversations with messengers from another planet.

   Interpersonal: 1 2 3 4 5 6 7 8 9 10
   Intercultural: 1 2 3 4 5 6 7 8 9 10
   Psychopathological: 1 2 3 4 5 6 7 8 9 10

10. A woman sees a counselor because she feels that she has a lot of difficulty making friends.

    Interpersonal: 1 2 3 4 5 6 7 8 9 10
    Intercultural: 1 2 3 4 5 6 7 8 9 10
    Psychopathological: 1 2 3 4 5 6 7 8 9 10

11. A man seeks help in trying to understand his teenage son's fixation with rock music. It appears that his son has trouble with absenteeism at school.

    Interpersonal: 1 2 3 4 5 6 7 8 9 10
    Intercultural: 1 2 3 4 5 6 7 8 9 10
    Psychopathological: 1 2 3 4 5 6 7 8 9 10

12. A man approaches a counselor with feelings of depression. He feels that his job is leading nowhere and that his occupational efforts are fruitless.

    Interpersonal: 1 2 3 4 5 6 7 8 9 10
    Intercultural: 1 2 3 4 5 6 7 8 9 10
    Psychopathological: 1 2 3 4 5 6 7 8 9 10

13. A 19-year-old sophomore complains to a counselor that she is being sexually harassed by her male professors. She claims that this has occurred throughout her academic life.

Interpersonal:	1	2	3	4	5	6	7	8	9	10
Intercultural:	1	2	3	4	5	6	7	8	9	10
Psychopathological:	1	2	3	4	5	6	7	8	9	10

14. A 32-year-old woman is reluctant to leave her parents' home to live on her own. She feels that to do so would be to lack filial responsibility.

Interpersonal:	1	2	3	4	5	6	7	8	9	10
Intercultural:	1	2	3	4	5	6	7	8	9	10
Psychopathological:	1	2	3	4	5	6	7	8	9	10

15. A 35-year-old man sees a counselor, complaining of chest and neck pains. He has sought medical help but has been diagnosed as medically "normal."

Interpersonal:	1	2	3	4	5	6	7	8	9	10
Intercultural:	1	2	3	4	5	6	7	8	9	10
Psychopathological:	1	2	3	4	5	6	7	8	9	10

16. A 31-year-old woman has had three sessions with a counselor; she has remained attentive to the counselor but has said very little about herself. She rarely volunteers any information during the sessions.

Interpersonal:	1	2	3	4	5	6	7	8	9	10
Intercultural:	1	2	3	4	5	6	7	8	9	10
Psychopathological:	1	2	3	4	5	6	7	8	9	10

17. An international student is confused about his feelings. He wishes to stay in the United States and pursue an academic career, yet his sense of nationalism and family unity have pressured him to consider returning to his native country.

Interpersonal:	1	2	3	4	5	6	7	8	9	10
Intercultural:	1	2	3	4	5	6	7	8	9	10
Psychopathological:	1	2	3	4	5	6	7	8	9	10

18. A 28-year-old woman is referred by her husband because she constantly uses prescription drugs to help her cope with day-to-day existence; the woman is aware of her drug use but denies that it affects her family life.

Interpersonal:	1	2	3	4	5	6	7	8	9	10
Intercultural:	1	2	3	4	5	6	7	8	9	10
Psychopathological:	1	2	3	4	5	6	7	8	9	10

19. A 22-year-old woman approaches a counselor, complaining that she cannot focus on relevant issues. She claims that her thinking has suddenly become "diffuse."

Interpersonal:	1	2	3	4	5	6	7	8	9	10
Intercultural:	1	2	3	4	5	6	7	8	9	10
Psychopathological:	1	2	3	4	5	6	7	8	9	10

20. A 20-year-old factory worker is referred to a counselor by his work supervisor. It appears that the man is lazy on the job and that his absenteeism is higher than average.

Interpersonal:	1	2	3	4	5	6	7	8	9	10
Intercultural:	1	2	3	4	5	6	7	8	9	10
Psychopathological:	1	2	3	4	5	6	7	8	9	10

Discuss whether students see the presenting problem as *primarily* a problem of interpersonal communication, a problem of intercultural contact, or a problem of pathology. When the questionnaire has been used previously, there has been a tendency for persons with *less* training and/or education to describe the presenting problem as *more* likely to be cultural and *less* likely to be pathological. Those with *more* training and/or education tended to describe the presenting problem as *more* likely to be pathological and *less* likely to be cultural.

Insight
Culturally different people will view the presenting problems from different perspectives.

CHAPTER 13

RESEARCH AND RESEARCH HYPOTHESES ABOUT EFFECTIVENESS IN INTERCULTURAL COUNSELING

The thirteenth chapter, by Norman D. Sundberg and David Sue, examines the research process for counselors doing dissertations or writing research proposals on multicultural issues. A rich collection of research hypotheses and designs are presented and discussed showing how to develop research on multicultural issues related to counseling and therapy.

Discussion Questions

1. What are the problems in striking a balance between overdifferentiation and underdifferentiation in cross-cultural research?

2. How would you determine the culturally different client's expectation about what will happen in counseling, and which variables would you emphasize?

3. How would you assess a counselor's communication style as appropriate or inappropriate for counseling across cultures?

4. How might you develop a client's intercultural attitudes and skills in counseling across cultures?

5. Which aspects of the client's external environment are particularly salient to counseling across cultures?

6. Discuss the viewpoint that all counselors from different cultures use more or less the same methods or pancultural common elements.

7. What are the best kinds of criteria to evaluate the effectiveness of intercultural counseling and why?

8. Why has there not been more research on the effectiveness of intercultural counseling?

9. How would you research "folk counseling" or "natural" systems of problem solving in another culture?

10. What do you predict for the future in research about cross-cultural counseling effectiveness?

Multiple Choice Questions

1. The greatest value in determining the conduciveness of traditional counseling theories and techniques under intercultural conditions lies in studying the effects of:
   a) unicultural values
   b) similarity-diversity
   c) counseling techniques
   d) research techniques

2. Three factors that will affect the entry into the counseling system of clients who are culturally different are:
   a) language/age/religion
   b) education/gender/religion
   c) language/religion/socialization
   d) none of the above

3. Counseling will be more effective for the intercultural client and counselor if *expectations* with regard to the goals of counseling are:
   a) minimal
   b) congruent
   c) of the counselor
   d) of the client

4. The use of Puerto Rican folktales as models of adaptive behavior is referred to as:
   a) play therapy
   b) cross-cultural art theory
   c) cuento therapy
   d) a and b

5. An intercultural client's preferred counseling characteristics are referred to as:
   a) counselor variable
   b) cross-cultural expectations
   c) client variable
   d) none of the above

6. Clients who are culturally different may operate from a cultural framework that has past, present, or future fields of action. This is referred to as:
   a) culture gap
   b) acculturation
   c) time orientation
   d) a and b

7. The questions "who does a client identify with," "whose judgment about worth and status are accepted," and "who will be important to the client in the future," refer to the client's:
   a) religion
   b) reference group or groups
   c) socialization process
   d) none of the above

8. A major factor in counseling foreign students for the "arena of future action" is whether or not the client intends to stay:
   a) in the host culture
   b) in counseling
   c) in school
   d) all of the above

9. An overriding caution in counseling an intercultural client is that the counselor should not treat the client as:
   a) any other client
   b) a foreigner
   c) a stereotype
   d) b and c

10. The effectiveness of intercultural counseling will be enhanced by the counselor's general sensitivity to communications, both verbal and nonverbal, and by a knowledge of _____ in other cultures.
    a) historical and social processes
    b) religious values
    c) levels of acculturation
    d) communication styles

Case Studies

1. A white female school counselor moved to Los Angeles from Ohio with her husband, who had accepted a principal's position at a high school. The counselor experienced culture shock when she met the parents of a Hispanic student who were concerned about their son's truancy problem. The parents spoke limited English, but enough to be able to communicate with those who did not speak Spanish.

Understanding the demographics of the school where she worked and in anticipation of working with Hispanic parents with limited English speaking ability, the counselor thought it would be beneficial to enroll in a Spanish class. For the next six months the counselor attended a Spanish course at a community college near her residence.

At work the counselor practiced her Spanish with students whenever possible and found that Hispanic students were less inhibited around her. On several occasions the counselor was able to speak Spanish with parents who spoke limited English. She noticed that speaking Spanish with the parents allowed them to feel relaxed and comfortable. The counselor realized that by being able to communicate in the language of her clients she was able to establish trust and rapport.

2. An Asian family who was experiencing difficulty with their oldest daughter met with a family therapist. The family informed the counselor that they did not approve of their daughter having boyfriends and found it difficult to get her to obey their rules.

The therapist spoke with the parents about relationships and what that meant to a teenage female. The therapist informed the parents that it would probably be best if the daughter could attend their next meeting so that they could all work out a solution together.

The parents were somewhat taken aback by what the therapist told them. They expressed to the therapist that they did not think it was possible for the family to meet. All that they wanted was for the therapist to tell them how to handle the situation.

Classroom Activities

PROJECTING INTO A GROUP

Objective

To help cross-culture workshop participants recognize differences in how they see groups by providing a picture of a group whose interaction can be interpreted in a variety of ways. Participants are encouraged to use photographs of groups/persons from different cultures.

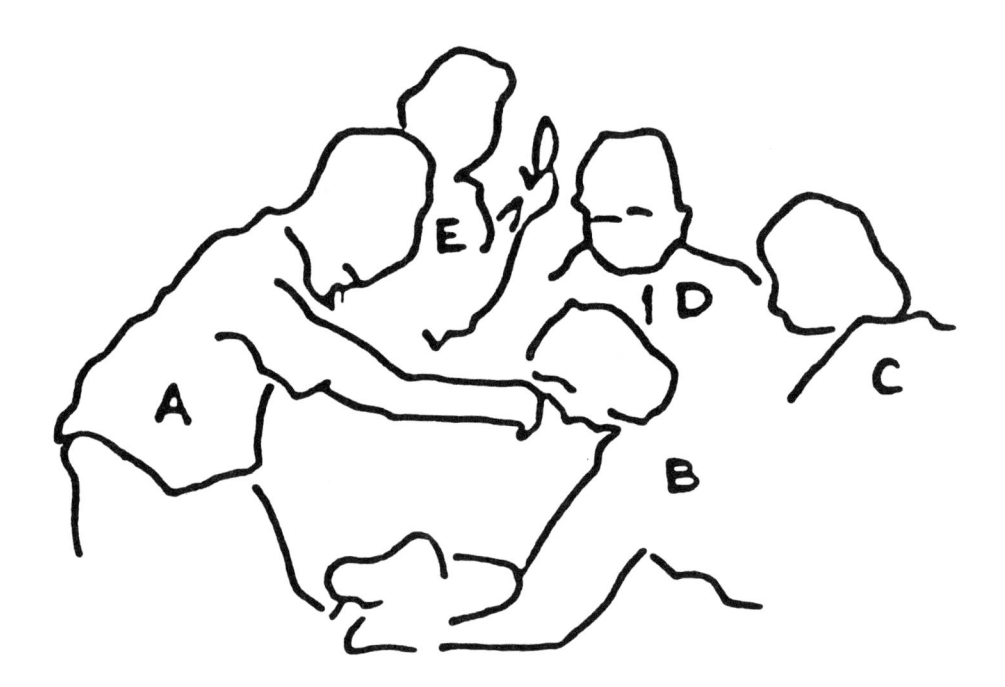

Developed by Murray Thomas, University of California, Santa Barbara

Procedure

1. Each participant is given a copy of the group picture.

2. Each member is asked to identify the persons in the picture according to their race and to give a brief description of what is happening.

3. Differences in response are discussed in terms of the cultural identity of the participants and the assumed roles of the group picture member.

Insight

A "multicultural picture" is worth a thousand words.

LUMP SUM

Adapted from "Lump-Sum: A Bargaining Simulation Game Design," by Marshall R. Singer and Paul B. Pedersen (Kuala Lumpur, Malaysia, 1970)

Objective

To demonstrate feelings, roles, and attitudes in a simulated situation of conflict among competing national interest groups.

Procedure

The size of groups may range from four to 12 individuals and the number of groups from four to six, each group representing a different culture. The simulated lump sum of money should be adequate to stimulate planning within groups and competition between groups. We recommend 10,000,000 units in either U.S. dollars or mixed currency representing the groups' national compositions. Simulate international consultations. Participant countries vie for aid from the United Nations' Special Fund, the International Monetary Fund, or some other reasonably authentic donor. One and a half hours plus debriefing and preparation should be allowed to complete the simulation.

1. The facilitator decides on the situation to be simulated, consulting participants if and whenever possible.

2. Participants are introduced to the interaction by the facilitator and are given a copy of the scenario to study.

3. "Interest groups" are formed either through assignment of roles by the facilitator or by having participants volunteer for membership in designated special interest groups, keeping all groups approximately equal in size.

4. Special interest groups meet separately to:
   a. elect a special interest group negotiator,
   b. decide on the overall division of funds with special attention to the sum their interest group plans to request for itself and prepare an argument defending their allocation both for all groups in general and for their own group in particular,
   c. decide on a strategy for securing their portion (i.e., the maximum they hope to obtain and the minimum for which they will settle in later negotiations),
   d. decide on bargaining strategies and possible coalitions of interest between groups to their mutual benefit.

   Groups may be allowed a minimum of 20 minutes and a maximum of an hour in which to develop their initial program strategy. The longer a group meets in its initial session, the stronger group identity tends to become and the less likely the group is to compromise. Because more learning seems to occur among groups that do not compromise, and thus lose the money, the more time individual groups can have in the initial session the better.

5. The first negotiation session takes place with each group's elected negotiator being placed at a bargaining table in such a way that he faces his constituency. Each negotiator will be given only three minutes to report on his delegation's specific proposal for allocation of the money. There must be no discussion among the representatives or debate from the floor while each negotiator defends his allocation within the three minutes.

6. The first consultation session allows negotiators to return to their groups and consult with the members (their own group and others if desired) on strategy, presentation, and changes in the group proposal. The consultation continues for 10 minutes. Private consultation and negotiations with other special interest groups is permitted at this time.

7. The second negotiation brings negotiators back to the bargaining table for at least 10 minutes but for no more than 15 minutes. This is the first public bargaining session where negotiators are allowed to speak and debate without restriction.

8. The second and last consultation session allows negotiators to return to their groups for 10 minutes. In the second consultation further modifications in each group's proposals can be made. Again, each group may wish to engage in private negotiations with other groups to secure their cooperation toward a solution.

9. The third negotiation session brings negotiators back to the bargaining table for the last time for a 20-minute period, unless the negotiators come to a unanimous agreement before that time. Negotiators must reach unanimous agreement in this session or lose the money.

10. After the simulation, a minimum of 20 minutes must be allowed for debriefing on the learning that has taken place through the simulation. Discussion should be oriented to the content level (articulation of information and the position of each simulated interest group by participants) and the process level (the interaction of individuals in this simulation as they approach bargaining negotiations and exercise power).

Sample Scenario

Instructions:
The following scenario is one that was used for a simulation done with students of education at the University of Malaya late in 1969. Six groups, representing the states of Malaysia, were used in that simulation . It is suggested that this scenario be adapted to the specifics of the simulation to be run and that copies of the adaptation be distributed to each of the participants. If duplication facilities are not available, the adaptation can be read to the entire group. The words in parentheses should be changed to suit the circumstances of the simulation, as it is being conducted. That is, if the setting of the simulation is special interest groups in New York instead of being an emergency meeting on educational planning for Malaysia by representatives of state assemblies (as it reads on the scenario presented below) the scenario might be entitled "Emergency Meeting of Representatives of Special Interest Groups in New York."

In the scenario below, participants were divided into six groups and were then presented with the scenario. The entire simulation was conducted in one day. It is also possible to run the simulation over two days. The timetable should be adjusted to suit the time constraints under which the simulation may have to operate, with one session devoted to preparation and a later session devoted to negotiations.

If the simulation is being conducted in a language other than English, the scenario should be translated into the language in which it will be conducted.

STRICTLY CONFIDENTIAL

EMERGENCY MEETING ON EDUCATIONAL PLANNING FOR MALAYSIA BY REPRESENTATIVES OF STATE ASSEMBLIES

You have been called together in this special emergency meeting to represent the unique interests of your (constituencies) in making an extremely important decision. The future of our (country) may depend on your decision today and the unique opportunity presented to us.

A representative of the (United Nations' Special Fund) has today informed me that because of bureaucratic oversight there is (U.S. $10,000,000) that has not been allocated in the budget for any specific project and is available for the use (of Malaysia) *provided* that you can make a rapid decision on allocation of those funds and inform (the Secretary-General of the United Nations in New York) by this afternoon. We have an open telephone line to (the Secretary-General's office) to notify him as soon as a decision is made. The representative apologized for the urgency of his request but the fiscal year for the (United Nations) ends tonight and all funds already appropriated but not allocated to specific projects by that time will revert to the (United Nations' General Fund) and will not be available for (Special Fund).

For the sake of speed and the fair allocation of the money, special representatives (from the various state assemblies of Malaysia) have been called together today to draw up a specific allocation of the money. The (United Nations) does not care how the money is allocated but (for the sake of national unity and the good of the whole country) they stipulate *absolutely* that you *must* come to a unanimous agreement on your decision within the time limit or lose the money.

(The United Nations) agrees to abide by whatever allocations you *unanimously* decide on within the next (90 minutes).

You are already divided into your (six state assembly) groupings:
1. (Sarawak-Sabah)
2. (Perak-Penang-Province Wellesley)
3. (Kelantan-Trengganu)
4. (Pahang-Johore)
5. (Negri Sembilan-Malacca)
6. (Kedah-Perlis)

For the sake of a speedy decision, each group will select its own negotiator, and the (six) negotiators will carry out the actual negotiations on allocation of the money.

Because only (90 minutes) can be allowed to reach a conclusion, we have established a timetable that *must* be rigidly adhered to. You will have adequate time to express the proposal of your delegations toward unanimous agreement. Although the actual negotiations will take place through your elected negotiator, you may, if the majority of the delegation is dissatisfied with his or her performance, replace your representative with someone else selected by the majority of your delegation.

Your timetable is as follows:

(20 minutes): Each delegation will meet together, settle among themselves who will be the negotiator representing them in the negotiations, and draw up specific plans for how the entire ($10,000,000) ought to be divided and allocated according to the needs of the entire (country) and the special concerns of your own (constituency).

(18 minutes): In the first negotiation session, each representative will be given three minutes to report on how his or her delegation proposes to allocate the money. There will be no discussion among the representatives, but each representative will be given an opportunity to explain the merits of his or her delegation's allocation of the money to the assembled company.

(10 minutes): In the first consultation session, representatives will go back to their own delegation for 10 minutes to consult with them on strategy, presentation, any changes in their proposals they may want to make, and private consultation with members of other groups.

(10 minutes): In the second negotiation session, representatives will present any modifications that may have been made on the basis of having heard the other representatives' proposals or on the basis of the consultations that have just taken place.

(10 minutes): In the second consultation, further modifications in each group's proposals can be made. Also, this is the time to consult again with other groups on any private compromises that may be proposed to secure their cooperation.

(20 minutes): In the third negotiation session, representatives will discuss and present their final and presumably unanimously-agreed-upon proposal on allocation of the ($10,000,000).

Insight

When this exercise was used in the past, those groups from or simulating dominant Western culture reached consensus but sacrificed principles while those from or simulating minority or non-Western culture did not reach consensus but evaluated their principles.

ANSWER KEY

MULTIPLE CHOICE QUESTIONS

Chapter 1	Chapter 2	Chapter 3	Chapter 4	Chapter 5	Chapter 6
1. c	1. a	1. d	1. c	1. c	1. c
2. d	2. c	2. c	2. b	2. c	2. d
3. c	3. c	3. d	3. b	3. d	3. c
4. b	4. d	4. c	4. d	4. c	4. d
5. c	5. d	5. b	5. b	5. a	5. d
6. a	6. d	6. d	6. c	6. c	6. c
7. d	7. c	7. d	7. b	7. c	7. d
8. a	8. d	8. c	8. b	8. c	8. c
9. c	9. c	9. d	9. c	9. a	9. c
10. d	10. b	10. c	10. c	10. b	10. a

Chapter 7	Chapter 8	Chapter 9	Chapter 10	Chapter 11	Chapter 12
1. c	1. d	1. c	1. d	1. c	1. b
2. c	2. b	2. b	2. d	2. d	2. b
3. b	3. a	3. d	3. c	3. b	3. c
4. c	4. b	4. c	4. d	4. d	4. d
5. b	5. b	5. c	5. b	5. b	5. d
6. d	6. c	6. c	6. b	6. c	6. d
7. d	7. c	7. b	7. a	7. b	7. c
8. d	8. d	8. d	8. a	8. a	8. b
9. c	9. d	9. c	9. a	9. d	9. d
10. a	10. d	10. d	10. d	10. a	10. c

Chapter 13
1. b
2. c
3. b
4. c
5. c
6. c
7. b
8. a
9. a
10. a